IMAGES
of America

BERKELEY
HEIGHTS

CHATHAM BRIDGE

SANDY HOOK

PASSAICVILLE

FRANKLIN PLACE

Summit

DUCKTOWN

HUNTLEY

MT. VERNON   ELKWOOD

DEANTOWN

TURKEY

OVERLOOK   EAST SUMMIT

WEST SUMMIT

TURKEYTOWN

FOUR CORNERS

BALTY ROLL HEIGHTS

POTTERS CORNER   **New Providence**

Springfield

MILLTOWN

ELLENOOR

MURRAY HILL   COUNTRYSIDE

BALTUSROL

SAYRE BRIDGE

LITTELS CORNER

PEPPERTOWN

BENDERS CORNER   GLENSIDE PARK

DEERFIELD

FRENCHTOWN

FELTVILLE DESERTED
PETER'S HILL   VILLAGE   SKY TOP   **Mountainside**   BRANCHVILLE

Berkeley Heights

BRANCH MILLS

BIRCH HILL

LOCUST GROVE

WOLF HILL   STONY HILL

BIRD'S CORNER   MORGAN'S HILL

UNION VILLAGE   LUCAS CORNERS

WYCHWOOD

PROSPECT HEIGHTS   GERMANTOWN

Cranfo

FREE ACRES

CRANETOWN

BROWNTOWN

Scotch   INDIAN FOREST   HUBBELL'S FOLLY

CRANEVIL
OAKLAND   FRENCH HOUSE

EDGEWOOD   **Garwood**   OAKWOOD

SCOT'S PLAIN

FANWOOD PARK   GRACELAND   **Westfield**   RIPLEY MANOR

Fanwood

CHERRY CORNER   PARK SLOPE

STONELEIGH PARK   ELMHURST   PICTON   INDIAN VILLAG

WOLF HARBOR

PARKWOOD

LENOX

NETHERWOOD

Plains   LAMBERTS MILLS

MILLTOWN

WILLOW GROVE   **Clark**

THE PLAINS   SCOTCHWOOD

PINCHGUT   SLEEPY HOLLOW

GOODMAN'S CROSSING

CENTRAL PARK   EVERGREEN

TWO BRIDGES

MADISON HILL

Plainfield   BLONDYN PLAINS

ALTON

ASH BROOK   HILLCREST

LARAMIE PARK

OAK RIDGE

EVONA

DOG CORNERS

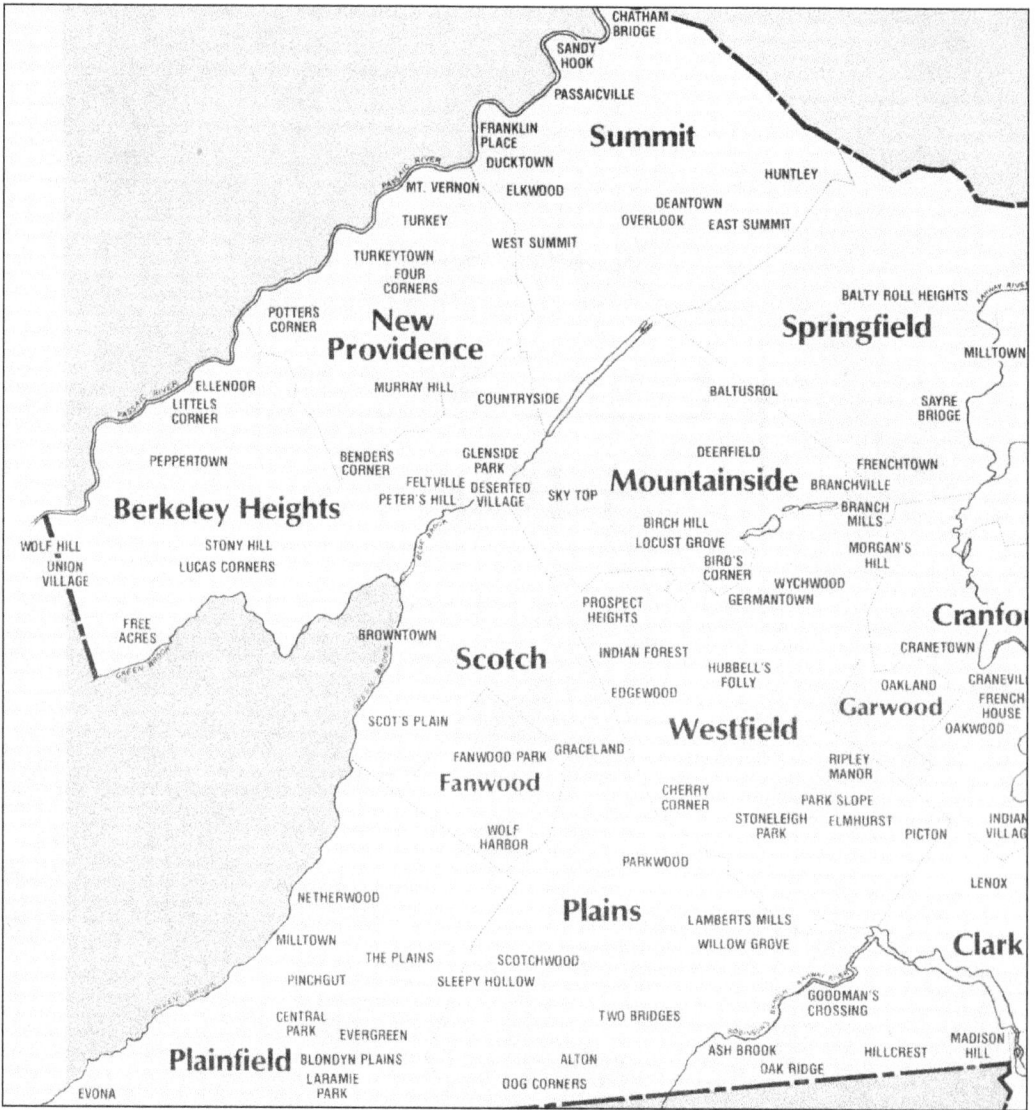

NEIGHBORHOOD NAMES IN AND AROUND BERKELEY HEIGHTS. After the English took New Jersey from the Dutch in 1664, the land we know as Berkeley Heights was included in the large township of Elizabethtown. At that time, New Providence, of which Berkeley Heights was a part, was called by the curious name of Turkey. (Yes, there were wild turkeys roaming the territory.) When an unfinished second-floor gallery collapsed in the Presbyterian church in 1750, the Turkey folk renamed their town New Providence as a way of thanking God for keeping everyone safe during the accident. In 1794 New Providence separated from Elizabethtown and joined Springfield Township, and in 1809 New Providence formed its own independent township. Another change occurred in 1899 when New Providence Borough split from the township; the Berkeley Heights section kept the name of New Providence Township. Finally, in 1952, Berkeley Heights citizens voted to officially call their community Berkeley Heights Township, bringing to an end the confusion of two neighboring New Providences. Many of the local section names have disappeared, but Deserted Village, Free Acres, Murray Hill, and Countryside have survived to the present time. (Union County Office of Cultural and Heritage Affairs, Division of Parks and Recreation; layout by L.P. Fuhro, 1981.)

IMAGES
of America

BERKELEY HEIGHTS

Virginia B. Troeger

ARCADIA
PUBLISHING

Published by Arcadia Publishing
Charleston, South Carolina

For all general information contact Arcadia Publishing at:
Telephone 843-853-2070
Fax 843-853-0044
E-mail sales@arcadiapublishing.com
For customer service and orders:
Toll-Free 1-888-313-2665

Visit us on the Internet at www.arcadiapublishing.com

To Trevor, Julia, and Jasmine
—Photographers of the Twenty-First Century—

ON THE COVER: A CHURCH REMEMBERED. Worshippers are gathered with their clergymen outside old Saint Mary's Stony Hill Roman Catholic Church after a combined service of holy communion and confirmation in 1910. Although the church was located just across the border in Watchung, it was founded in the 1840s by Berkeley Heights residents, especially early settlers from Germany. To the great sadness of local residents, this cherished sanctuary, which represented the origins of the Roman Catholic Church in this area, was torn down in 1974. Saint Mary's Stony Hill Cemetery remains on the property. *See photographs on pages 114–115.* (Anne Del Duca Bosefskie.)

Contents

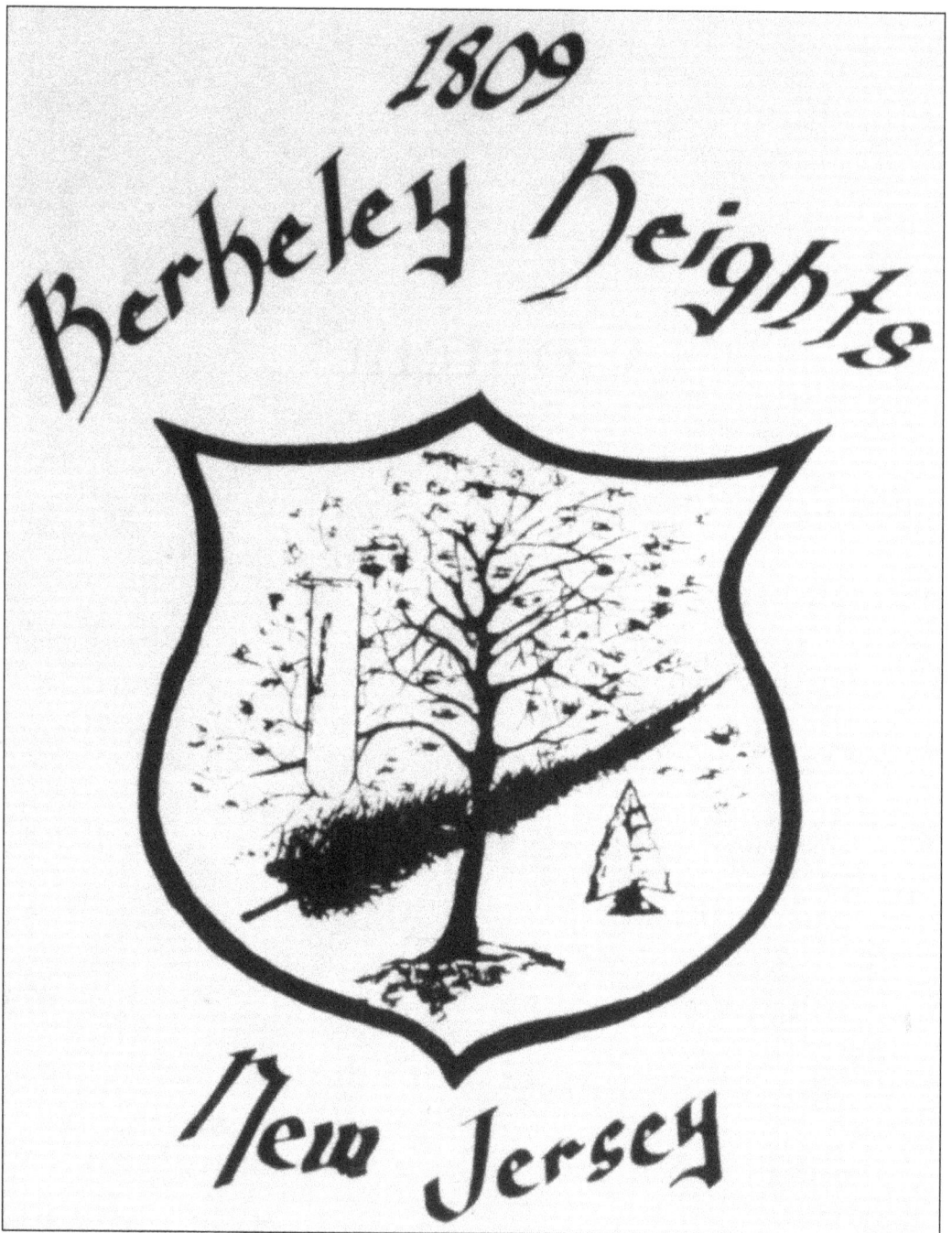

OFFICIAL TOWNSHIP SEAL. In the spring of 1960 the Berkeley Heights Township Committee sponsored a contest in the schools to select a township seal. Patricia Jean Taylor, an eighth grader at Columbia School, designed the winning seal, which is used on official vehicles, uniforms, stationery, and the township flag. Patricia's central symbol is the dogwood tree, which is native to this area. The test tube, the quill, and the arrowhead represent the importance of scientific research, education, and the heritage of the Lenni-Lenape Indians in the growth and development of the township of Berkeley Heights. (Rita Ragno.)

6

Introduction

After Trevor, my first grandchild, was born, my daughter Janice and I wondered which of our family members he might resemble. We looked closely at the pictures in our family baby albums and watched a composite video of Trevor's dad's early years. We spotted a familiar smile here, a similar tilt of the head there. But we noticed something else, too. Although the photographs themselves had not changed, Janice, now a mother, and I, a grandmother, were bringing new perspectives to these images.

A photograph album of a town isn't very different. It's simply a family collection encompassing a wider range of people and places. As you view these vintage pictures from the 1880s to the early 1960s, share them with others—and if you have stories of "the good old days," tell them also. Whether you're a lifelong resident or a new one, young or not so young, may this book link you in different ways at different times to days past, days present, and days to come in our flourishing community of Berkeley Heights, New Jersey.

Virginia Bergen Troeger
July 1996

Acknowledgments

I knew that working on this book would not be a one-woman project, but I was surprised and gratified by the ever-widening circle of people who contributed to its completion. First I must remember the late Frederick S. Best, who contributed his large collection of photographs to the Berkeley Heights Historical Society, and Hazel DeForest Rose, who chronicled the history of Runnells Hospital.

Helen Tyler, president of the Berkeley Heights Historical Society, helped me look through the society's collection of photographs, sharing her broad knowledge and stories of the past. Gail Shaffer, Mildred Shaffer, and Marjorie Baranoski provided me with photographs, names, and lore from far back in the history of Berkeley Heights.

Historian Dave "Bo" Bosefskie proved to be a fountain of facts about our town and a wonderful source of photographs from his own files and from the collections of members of his family, Angela Del Duca Sampson, Ernie DeFronzo, and Bo's mother, Anne Del Duca Bosefskie. Bo also led me to Tom Delia and Steve Imbimbo, who unearthed a long-unopened box of photographs of street scenes at the water treatment department.

My friend and colleague Rita Ragno kindly lent me a multimedia history of Berkeley Heights that she had prepared some years ago. I am also indebted to George Bebbington of Warren for making available photographs of AT&T and for arranging the release of historic photographs of Bell Labs with Renzo deCarlo of Lucent Technologies.

Other individuals and organizations who provided vintage pictures and answered my many questions include: Ida Bartholomew; Stephanie Bakos, Laura Fuhro, and other staff members of the Berkeley Heights Public Library; the Berkeley Heights Woman's Club; Rich Bower of the Berkeley Heights Rescue Squad; Rosemary Campano of Little Flower Church; Bob Craig of the New Jersey Historic Preservation Office; Anthony Delia; Carol Drake Friedman; Lawrence P. Fuhro of the Cranford Historical Society; Caryl Hannemann; George Hawley of the Newark Public Library; Laurel Hessing of Free Acres; Holly Hoffman of the Trailside Museum Association; *The Independent Press*; Ludmilla and Barnaby Kent; Kate Middleton; the New Providence Historical Society; Florence "Pat" Risden; Nan Rogers; Joan Rotondi; Margaret "Peggy" Salisbury of Runnells Hospital; Charles Shallcross of the Union County Historical Society; Jerome Shaw; Alan A. Siegel; the Summit Historical Society; the Summit Public Library; Joan Rosé Thomas; Nadine Tokash; Frances Truppi; Dan Bernier, Barbara Fuller, Debra Judd, and Linda McTeague of the Union County Office of Cultural and Heritage Affairs; the Watchung Public Library; and Mary Lou Weller.

Many, many thanks must go to my husband Walter, Janice and Ernie Lettieri, Joanne Troeger, and Scott Lavender, who read the manuscript, made helpful suggestions, and rescued me from computer glitches. Working in absentia, Cindy and Eric Gullikson of Oakland, California, offered advice via e-mail and the telephone. Of course, I am grateful also for those photographers of the past who made this book possible in the first place.

One

On the Avenue, Springfield Avenue

SPRINGFIELD AVENUE, c. 1900. This main street of Berkeley Heights appeared on many early area maps. It was a major trail running east-west during the time that the Lenni-Lenape traversed the land. On a 1741 map, Springfield Avenue was listed as "Turkey Road" and has also been called "Valley Road to New Providence," "Liberty Street," and the "Farmer's Turnpike." On this old postcard, the Del Duca General Store at the corner of Springfield and Plainfield Avenues can be seen on the left. (Gail Shaffer.)

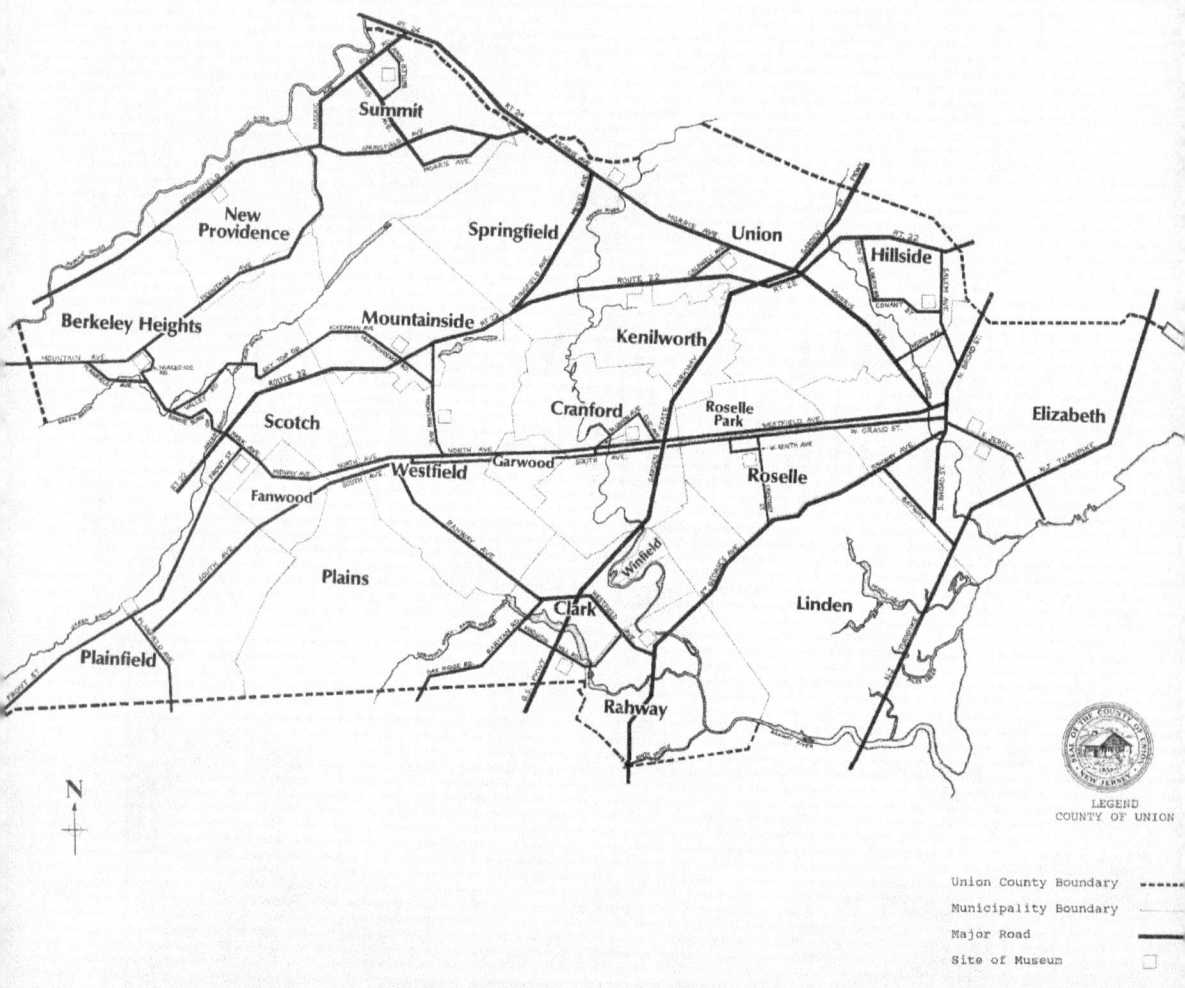

UNION COUNTY. This contemporary map shows the location of the 6.19 square miles of Berkeley Heights Township in the western corner of Union County. The township borders on Somerset and Morris Counties and extends to the Summit city line. The highest point in the county, 560 feet above sea level, is located in Berkeley Heights. (Union County Office of Cultural and Heritage Affairs, Division of Parks and Recreation; layout by L.P. Fuhro.)

NATHANIEL SMITH HOUSE, 1899. This pre-Revolutionary home, built *c.* 1740 on Springfield Avenue, is on both the State and National Registers of Historic Places. Frederick and Lois Best purchased the property in 1945 and lovingly preserved and restored their home. When Mr. Best died in 1995, his wife sold the house, which remains an enduring local landmark. (Rita Ragno.)

CRANE-DAY HOMESTEAD, *c.* 1885. Early settler Joseph Crane purchased land on Springfield Avenue in 1764 for his family home. His daughter-in-law, Betsey Mulford Crane, kept a diary between 1824 and 1828 which has provided many details about the life of this hardworking, Methodist family who farmed the land here years ago. (Rita Ragno.)

SIDE VIEW, CRANE-DAY HOUSE, c. 1900. The lady on the right may be stopping for a neighborly chat after bicycling about town. It must have been quite a challenge, however, to cycle along the hilly byways wearing a leg-of-mutton sleeved dress and bowler hat! (Berkeley Heights Historical Society.)

CRANE-DAY HOUSE, c. 1950. This historic dwelling remained in the Crane-Day family until the death of Betsey Mulford Crane's youngest daughter, Elizabeth Crane Day, in 1911. Mabel Bartholomew (pictured above) and her husband purchased the house in the 1940s as a summer home. Because later owners found the price of restoration too costly, the house was demolished in 1967. (Ida Bartholomew.)

PUBLIC SALE!

MR. MILLER, - AUCTIONEER.

The subscriber will dispose of at public auction at the Day Homestead, in the Borough of New Providence, on

TUESDAY, MAY 25, '09

PERSONAL PROPERTY, TO WIT:

BARN AND A COW SHED,

two buildings to be removed within thirty days after day of sale.

UPHOLSTERED SURREY

2-seat Sleigh, 2-seat Carriage, Single Harness, Plow Harness,

ONE-HORSE FARM WAGON,

and Hay Rigging, Cultivator, Acme and Tooth Harrows, Hay and Corn Cutter, Corn Sheller, Grain Cradle, Scythe, Large Vise, Garden Tools, Hammer, Saw, Dog House, &c., &c.

HOUSEHOLD GOODS:

Piano, Large Extension Table, pine top Dining Table, 2 Kitchen Tables, 2 Dog Chairs

LOUNGE, SOLID BLACK WALNUT BEDSTEAD,

3 other Bedsteads, Box Spiral Bedsprings, Wire Bedsprings, 2 Wash Stands, Pillows, Spring Cot with Mattress, 2 Bureaus with mirrors, Large Mahogany Bureau,

SINGER SEWING MACHINE,

Hall Hat Rack, Rochester, Hanging and Bracket Lamps, 9 yds Ingrain Carpet, Looking Glass, Toilet Articles, Quilting Frame, Wash Bench, Tub and Washing Machine, Cylinder Stove, Sausage Cutter, Carpenter Chest, Pots, Kettles, Dishes, &c. Sale to commence at one P M sharp TERMS CASH Other conditions will be given on day of sale by

EARLY GARAGE SALE, 1909. Not only was Franklin Day selling the usual household items, he was also hoping to find buyers for his barn, cow shed, and dog house! (Rita Ragno.)

PINE TREE INN, c. 1910. One of several inns that opened in town in the early 1900s, this Springfield Avenue landmark continues to this day as the elegant Auberge Swiss Restaurant. The front dining rooms of Auberge are the original Pine Tree Inn rooms. Though not visible here, the venerable pine tree, which also still stands, must have been a small sapling to the left of the inn. (Bo Bosefskie.)

SPRINGFIELD AND SNYDER AVENUES, 1914. The Pine Tree Inn, a popular tavern and meeting place, stands at right partially hidden by trees. During their summer vacations, city folk looked upon Berkeley Heights as a rural retreat and filled its small hotels and guest houses. (Berkeley Heights Historical Society.)

PINE TREE INN POSTCARD, *c.* 1950. With its stately namesake growing taller and sturdier, the Pine Tree Inn moved into the post-World War II era featuring two cocktail bars and that wonder of wonders, television! (Anthony Delia.)

PEPPERTOWN, *c.* 1910. One of the Italian families that grew peppers in the township was the Petrone family. Frank, Agnese, and their children are shown here with some hired help and a bountiful crop. When townsfolk noticed colorful peppers drying in the autumn sun in the center of town off Springfield Avenue, they nicknamed the area "Peppertown." (Bo Bosefskie.)

DEINLEIN EXTENDED FAMILY, 1902. Gustave Deinlein (second from left), one of the area's first German settlers, is shown here with his wife, children, and other relatives outside the Del Duca Store beneath the Bell Telephone pay station sign. When Berkeley Heights formed its own governing body in 1899, Gustave Deinlein served as the constable and as a road overseer. (Bo Bosefskie.)

DEL DUCA GENERAL STORE, c. 1902. This emporium at the corner of Springfield and Plainfield Avenues kept townsfolk supplied with many household items and had the only telephone in town. When a resident received a phone call, a store clerk would deliver the message, which was always important news: sometimes good, sometimes bad. No one called just to chat! (Bo Bosefskie.)

16

DEL DUCA GENERAL STORE, *c.* 1920. Signs for Rising Sun Lager Beer (*see opposite page*) have now given way to signs advertising Castle's Ice Cream and Coca-Cola. (Angela Sampson.)

FIRST TRAFFIC SIGNAL, *c.* 1930. Since traffic was already picking up at the corner of Springfield and Plainfield Avenues, the first traffic light in the township was installed at this intersection during the 1930s. The first policeman in town, D.V. Russo Jr. (left), operated the signal in front of Crabby's Tavern, which had replaced the Del Duca General Store of yesteryear. *See also page 69.* (Bo Bosefskie.)

ROMANO HOMESTEAD, 559 SPRINGFIELD AVENUE, c. 1910. Still part of the town's landscape, this house was built by Peter Romano who moved to Berkeley Heights from Brooklyn. Peter arrived in the United States from Naples, Italy, when he was seven years old. He and his wife, Rose Acunzo Romano, raised their twelve children in this house. (Mary Lou Weller.)

PROUD GRANDDAD, c. 1910. Grandfather Michelangelo Acunzo, Rose Romano's father, visits with five of his grandchildren outside the Romano home on Springfield Avenue. (Mary Lou Weller.)

FRANK A. ROMANO HARDWARE, 1924. Typical of many shopkeepers of the time, Peter Romano's son Frank maintained his hardware (and candy!) store in his home. Looking every bit a woman of the 1920s in her knee-length skirt and cloche hat, Margaret Romano Landwehr enjoys the sunshine outside the family store. Although the front of the house has changed through the years, this sturdy cement block building remains almost as it was constructed. Other buildings in town were also built with these rusticated blocks because the factory producing them was located on the site of the present town hall. One can only wonder about the meaning of the sign on the door which reads, "Love's Greatest Mistake!" *See also pages 25, 56–57.* (Mary Lou Weller.)

DEL DUCA GREENHOUSES, c. 1930. A.M. Del Duca established his flower-growing business on Springfield Avenue in 1907. Born in Italy in 1880, he arrived in the United States six years later. After gaining experience in the nursery business at L.B. Coddington's and Nason's in Murray Hill, he successfully branched out on his own. At left is the Venezia homestead. (Bo Bosefskie.)

CARNATION GREENHOUSE, c. 1940. Employees at Del Duca's Florist didn't have to stop to smell the roses; they were surrounded by sweet-scented carnations all the time! A.M. Del Duca (second from left) grew mainly cut roses, carnations, and delphiniums for the New York market, but also grew vegetable and flower plants for local gardeners. *See also pages 64–65.* (Angela Sampson.)

PROCESSION OF MOUNT CARMEL SOCIETY, *c.* 1915. The Mount Carmel Society was founded by Maria Venezia and others in 1909 to commemorate the Virgin Mary on her feast day, July 16. In the early years, Mrs. Venezia organized a procession of Catholic girls wearing white dresses and carrying banners to old Saint Mary's Stony Hill Church for a mass. Every July 16, Mount Carmel Society members continue the tradition with a parade through the downtown area featuring the original banner and a float carrying a statue of the Virgin Mary. Spectators often attach contributions to the streamers and receive scapulars. The Mount Carmel Society uses the proceeds from the fair to fund many township projects and a scholarship to a Governor Livingston High School graduating senior. (Bo Bosefskie.)

VENEZIA HOMESTEAD, 1910. When James Venezia arrived from Italy in 1884, there were about twenty-four families in Berkeley Heights. He purchased 18 acres of farmland on Springfield Avenue and built this house where he and his wife, Maria Del Duca, brought up their eight children. Along with farming and storekeeping, he worked as a foreman in the Coddington Greenhouses in Murray Hill. (Rita Ragno.)

VENEZIA PROPERTY, 1930. The horse and wagon have given way to an automobile, new rooms have been added to the house, and greenhouses have cropped up in the twenty years since the photograph at the top of the page was taken. This early dwelling still remains in the Venezia family. In 1945 Leona and Charles Roll opened the Berkeley Florist next door, a thriving business to this day. (Bo Bosefskie.)

22

HATS, HATS, HATS! 1914. Whatever happened to the flowered and ruffled attire worn by women until after World War I? These creations are being modeled by ladies of the Del Duca, Venezia, and Oechsner families. The lone male peeking through the finery is Joseph Del Duca, and the lady on the far right, the only person prepared for a sudden shower, is Mrs. Roland Parker, whose husband served as township clerk. (Ernie DeFronzo.)

ALL ON AN APRIL SUNDAY. Venezia family members, probably just back from church, gather outside their barn on Springfield Avenue with one of their four-footed friends on Sunday, April 2, 1933. (Ernie DeFronzo.)

VENEZIA WASH HOUSE. Cousins Walter Pedersen (left) and Ernie DeFronzo take a break from helping Aunt Mildred Venezia on a September day in 1936. The boys may have carried water to the wash house for doing the week's laundry. *See photographs on pages 62–63 and 66.* (Ernie DeFronzo.)

TOWNLEY'S BRIDGE, 1910. This postcard shows the intersection of Springfield Avenue and the Passaic and Delaware Branch of the Lackawanna Railroad crossing the Passaic River at the Gillette town line. The bridge was named for David H. Townley who lived nearby. (Bo Bosefskie.)

GATEMAN PETER ROMANO, *c.* 1915. Springfield Avenue resident Peter Romano opened and closed the railroad gates for ten years at Townley's Bridge. (Mary Lou Weller.)

RAILROAD CROSSING, 1925. A sign informs travelers on Springfield Avenue at the Gillette border of the hours when a flagman or gateman would be on duty. (Berkeley Heights Historical Society.)

LOOKING WEST ON THE AVENUE, c. 1925. For some years in the early 1900s, traffic had slowed on the stretch of Springfield Avenue west of New Providence because of a lack of improvements. In 1924 that part of the road was rebuilt with concrete, and Springfield Avenue again became a well-used road for those traveling from the Delaware River to Newark. (Berkeley Heights Historical Society.)

GILLETTE OVERPASS UNDER CONSTRUCTION. In 1936 the old wooden bridge on Springfield Avenue over the Passaic River was replaced by a concrete overpass, making the gateman's job at this crossing a thing of the past. (Bo Bosefskie.)

26

Two

"The Daily Life Must Be Spent Out of Doors"

COUNTY CHILDREN AT RISK, c. 1925. Exercising with weights outside the children's building at the Bonnie Burn Sanatorium in Berkeley Heights, these young patients are diligently practicing one of the important doctrines concerning tuberculosis given in *Rules for Patients*: "The daily life must be spent out of doors." In 1955, the Bonnie Burn Sanatorium was renamed the John E. Runnells Hospital for Chest Diseases. (Bo Bosefskie.)

FULLERTON PROPERTY, LOOKING NORTH, c. 1910. The Henry S. Fullerton estate in Berkeley Heights was one of several locations considered by the Union County Board of Chosen Freeholders for a county tuberculosis hospital. Some thought the land too remote but others overruled, citing the fresh mountain air, a sparkling brook, proximity to the Scotch Plains trolley . . . and the price was right! (Bo Bosefskie.)

FULLERTON HUNTING LODGE, c. 1910. Henry S. Fullerton, a Wall Street broker, country gentleman, and town father, sold his 146-acre estate in Berkeley Heights to the Union County Board of Freeholders in 1910 for approximately $13,000 to build the county tuberculosis hospital. This may be Mr. Fullerton himself standing in front of one of the many outbuildings on his extensive property. (Bo Bosefskie.)

FULLERTON HOMESTEAD, c. 1910. The local townsfolk felt outraged and betrayed when they found out that Henry S. Fullerton had sold his property for a TB hospital. What had caused Mr. Fullerton to bring this feared, contagious disease to their very doorsteps? One neighbor was so disturbed that he called in a carpenter to board up three sides of his open bucket well and install a door on the fourth side to prevent contamination of the water! In 1912 the county hospital, called the Bonnie Burn (a Scottish phrase meaning "pretty stream") Sanatorium, was opened and ready for patients. Mr. Fullerton's house (shown here) served as the superintendent's residence until the 1950s. (Bo Bosefskie.)

JOHN E. RUNNELLS, M.D., c. 1959. Born in Granby, Quebec, Canada, in 1876, Dr. Runnells came to the United States when he was twenty-two to study medicine. After graduating from Tufts Medical School, he practiced at several New England sanatoriums before joining Bonnie Burn in 1912, where he served as the superintendent and medical director until his retirement in 1959. (Bo Bosefskie.)

HAZEL DEFOREST ROSE, c. 1912. Miss Rose, seated on the rustic footbridge that connected a wooded island in the pond to the main grounds of Bonnie Burn, was hired as Dr. John E. Runnells' secretary when the hospital opened. She later served as assistant superintendent, retiring in 1957. (Bo Bosefskie.)

ADMINISTRATION BUILDING AND STAFF, 1912. In her unpublished history of the Bonnie Burn Sanatorium, Hazel DeForest Rose wrote that Dedication Day, November 18, 1912, was ". . . a memorable occasion. Hundreds visited the grounds and buildings. . . . The law requiring counties to care for their tuberculous had only been passed a short time before, and Union County was among the first to respond. We had labored for weeks to get all the buildings ready for occupancy . . . And so the stage was set—the Dedication was held, and we were ready for our first patient. I remember so well our first patient. He was a young man who was transferred to us from Saranac Lake and remained with us for several months." (Gail Shaffer.)

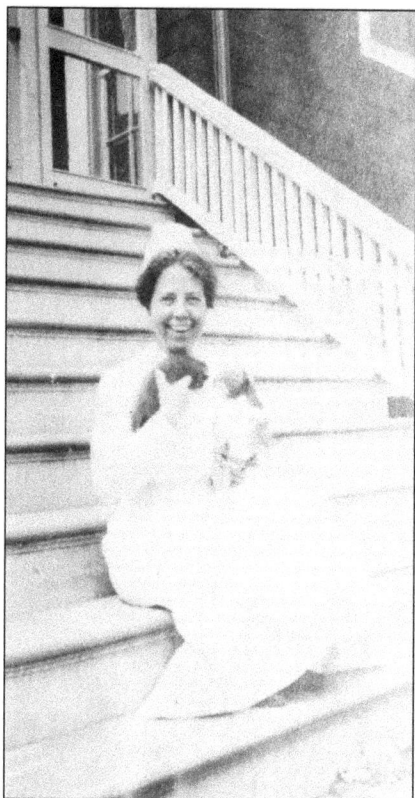

ALICE E. OSBORNE, c. 1913. The first trained nurse to join the Bonnie Burn staff, a smiling Miss Osborne poses on the steps of the administration building with two furry buddies. (Bo Bosefskie.)

HOSPITAL BILL, 1912. A Bonnie Burn patient's bill shows the total charges for one month, which were to be paid in advance. For many years the hospital's mailing address was a Scotch Plains post office box. The address was changed to Berkeley Heights in 1960. (Bo Bosefskie.)

HOSPITAL STAFF DINING ROOM, 1912. Gracious dining was the order of the day when Bonnie Burn first opened, but this room was later converted to office space as the hospital expanded. (Bo Bosefskie.)

BONNIE BURN MEDICAL BUILDING, 1921. The outdoor environment prescribed for tuberculosis patients is evident here; a ramp connects the medical building to the open sun deck at the rear of the "K" building, which housed one hundred patients at that time. (Bo Bosefskie.)

PREVENTORIUM, *c.* 1920. The children's building was dedicated in the spring of 1918 to care for children diagnosed as pretuberculous. It provided rooms for ninety-six youngsters and their nurses. The board of managers and staff were especially proud of this building because Bonnie Burn was one of the first county sanatoriums in New Jersey to build a preventorium. (Bo Bosefskie.)

SCHOOL AT BONNIE BURN, *c.* 1920. Young Union County patients learn their reading, writing, and arithmetic on the hospital grounds in one of the two classrooms in the preventorium. (Bo Bosefskie.)

WINTER DAY AT BONNIE BURN, *c.* 1920. Hospitalized children romp in the sun and snow outside the preventorium. Often whole families would reside together as patients. Fathers and mothers were housed in the men's and women's dormitories, the pretuberculous children in the preventorium, and children with active TB in the "baby shack." (Bo Bosefskie.)

SUMMER DAY AT BONNIE BURN, *c.* 1930. Young patients are dressed to soak up the sunshine and fresh, clean air of the Watchung Mountains. As the years passed, new medicines replaced the emphasis on outdoor living and wholesome food as the primary treatments for TB. (Bo Bosefskie.)

BONNIE BURN NURSES, c. 1920. Nurses in a residential hospital such as Bonnie Burn— where patients usually stayed for months—must have dispensed much tender loving care and words of comfort to both children and adults along with their prescribed medications. (Rita Ragno.)

BONNIE BURN ADMINISTRATION BUILDING, 1932. After the structure was remodeled in 1929, Hazel DeForest Rose wrote that "the whole building was refloored and redecorated, until it emerged a glorified Administration Building . . . The old kitchen has been remodeled into a spacious, light, and fully equipped Linen Room, and the left wing became a beautiful Recreation Room for the physicians and nurses." (Bo Bosefskie.)

36

OFFICE STAFF AT BONNIE BURN, 1932. After the daringly short skirts of the 1920s, women of the 1930s often made their fashion statement wearing softly ruffled dresses with longer, flowing hemlines. (Bo Bosefskie.)

A DREAM COME TRUE, 1932. The more than 120 children at Bonnie Burn must have been ready to jump right in when the new swimming pool opened in 1932 in this sylvan setting near the superintendent's residence. (Bo Bosefskie.)

NURSING STAFF, c. 1950. Though their skirts no longer covered their ankles, Bonnie Burn nurses looked crisp and spotless in their starched caps and uniforms, white stockings, and sturdy walking oxfords. Some years later, wash-and-wear fabrics and pants suits would transform nurses' traditional dress. (Bo Bosefskie.)

BONNIE BURN MAIN ENTRANCE, c. 1950. These stone gates were built in 1925 as a memorial to Dr. William Murray of Plainfield, the first president of the hospital's board of managers. Hazel DeForest Rose described his death as "a sad day for the sanatorium, for the work had always been very close to his heart." (Bo Bosefskie.)

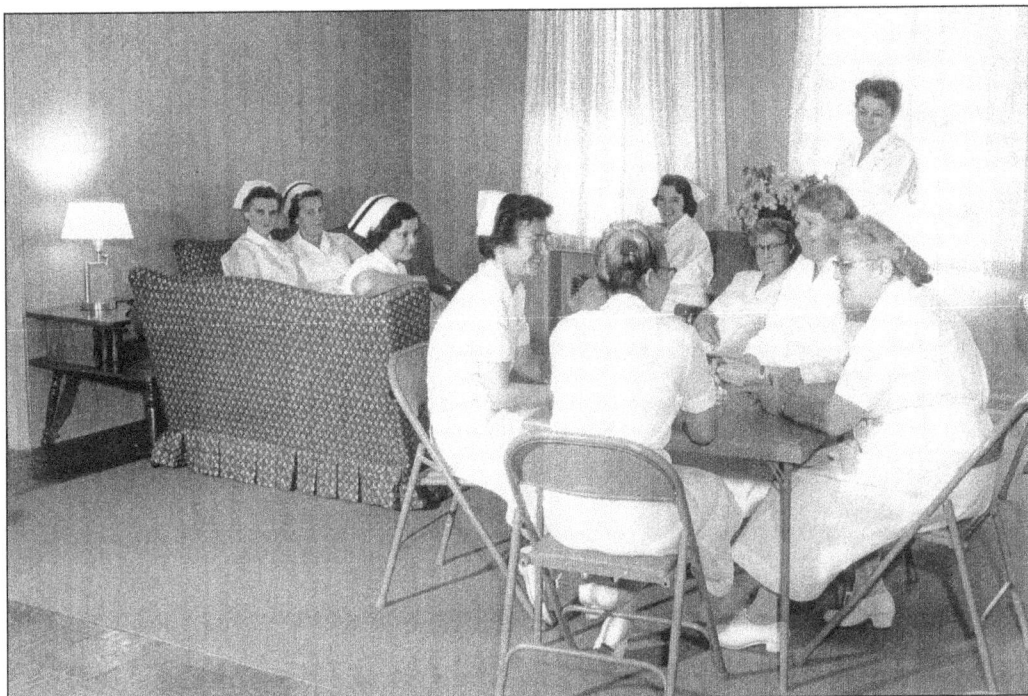

R AND R, c. 1960. The nursing staff gathers in their lounge for a few minutes of rest and relaxation before their next round of duties. (Bo Bosefskie.)

WATERFALL AND BROOK, 1956. This "pretty stream" or "bonnie burn" was one of the natural elements of the property that first attracted the Union County committee searching for a hospital site. (Bo Bosefskie.)

ROSE HALL, c. 1960. Built in 1956, the new nurses' residence was named in honor of the hospital's first assistant superintendent, Hazel DeForest Rose. Annual hospital reports from the early 1950s stressed the need for a modern nurses' home to enable Runnells to attract qualified medical personnel at a time when new hospitals were opening in the area. (Newark Public Library.)

CENTENNIAL FLOAT, 1957. Runnells Hospital joined the parade celebrating the 100th anniversary of Union County, the youngest New Jersey county. Before 1857, the county had been part of Essex County. (Bo Bosefskie.)

40

RUNNELLS BUILDINGS, 1955. The second floor of the auditorium (right) was used for occupational therapy for many years, while movies were shown and programs, often presented by the patients themselves, took place on the first floor. The recreation building stands at left. (Bo Bosefskie.)

HALF-CENTURY OF SERVICE, 1962. Honored guests congregated on the lawn of the administration building on October 12, 1962, for the flag-raising ceremony commemorating fifty years of medical service by Runnells Hospital to the citizens of Union County. (Bo Bosefskie.)

HIGHLANDERS TAKE THE FIELD, 1962. The Governor Livingston Regional High School Band performed during Runnells' 50th anniversary flag-raising ceremony. In the 1980s the John E. Runnells Hospital for Chest Diseases was closed, and the county property below Route 78 was sold to industry. In 1990 a new facility, Runnells Specialized Hospital, opened on 45 acres of county property adjoining the original location. (Bo Bosefskie.)

Three

The Labs

SITE OF BELL LABS, MURRAY HILL, 1930. In 1925 the Bell Telephone System formed Bell Labs to serve as its scientific center with headquarters in New York City. Five years later the company purchased this property in the Murray Hill section of Berkeley Heights from Niemants Nursery to build a much larger, state-of-the-art facility to meet the growing demands of technology. (Property of AT&T Archives, Reprinted with permission of AT&T.)

AERIAL VIEW OF BELL LABS PROPERTY, 1930. In a little more than a decade from this time, the quiet, farming community of Berkeley Heights would find itself the center of world-class scientific achievements as the home of Bell Telephone Laboratories, which opened in 1942. (George Bebbington.)

LABS IN WARTIME. In 1943 the army demonstrated an anti-aircraft gun on the Murray Hill grounds. The gun is controlled by an electronic box called a "director" which is operated by the soldiers on the far side of the gun. This system was used during World War II as a defense against enemy aircraft. (Property of AT&T Archives, Reprinted with permission of AT&T.)

TELLES CERAMIC LABORATORY, MURRAY HILL, 1946. (Property of AT&T Archives, Reprinted with permission of AT&T.)

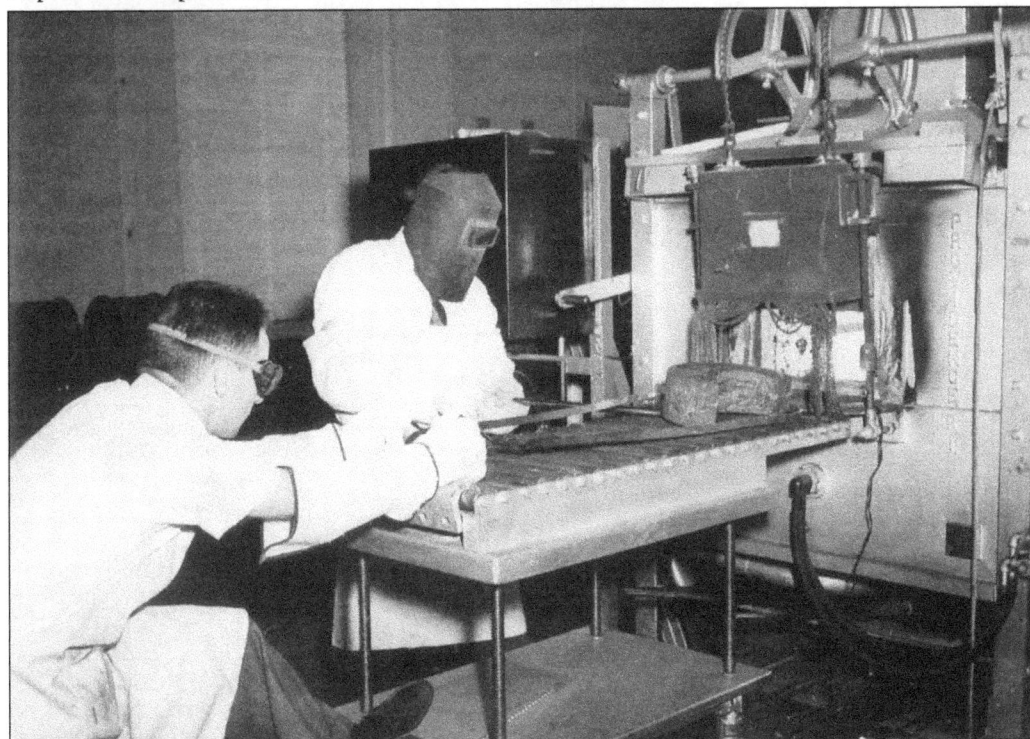

METALLURGICAL LAB, 1951. Murray Hill employees P.H. Schmitt (left) and F.J. Schnettler remove a permanent magnet from the furnace. (Property of AT&T Archives, Reprinted with permission of AT&T.)

GLASS-BLOWING SHOP, MURRAY HILL, 1955. (Property of AT&T Archives, Reprinted with permission of AT&T.)

SAFETY FIRST! Murray Hill employees test Bell Labs' fire-fighting equipment during a fire brigade refresher course on August 8, 1950. (Property of AT&T Archives; Reprinted with permission of AT&T.)

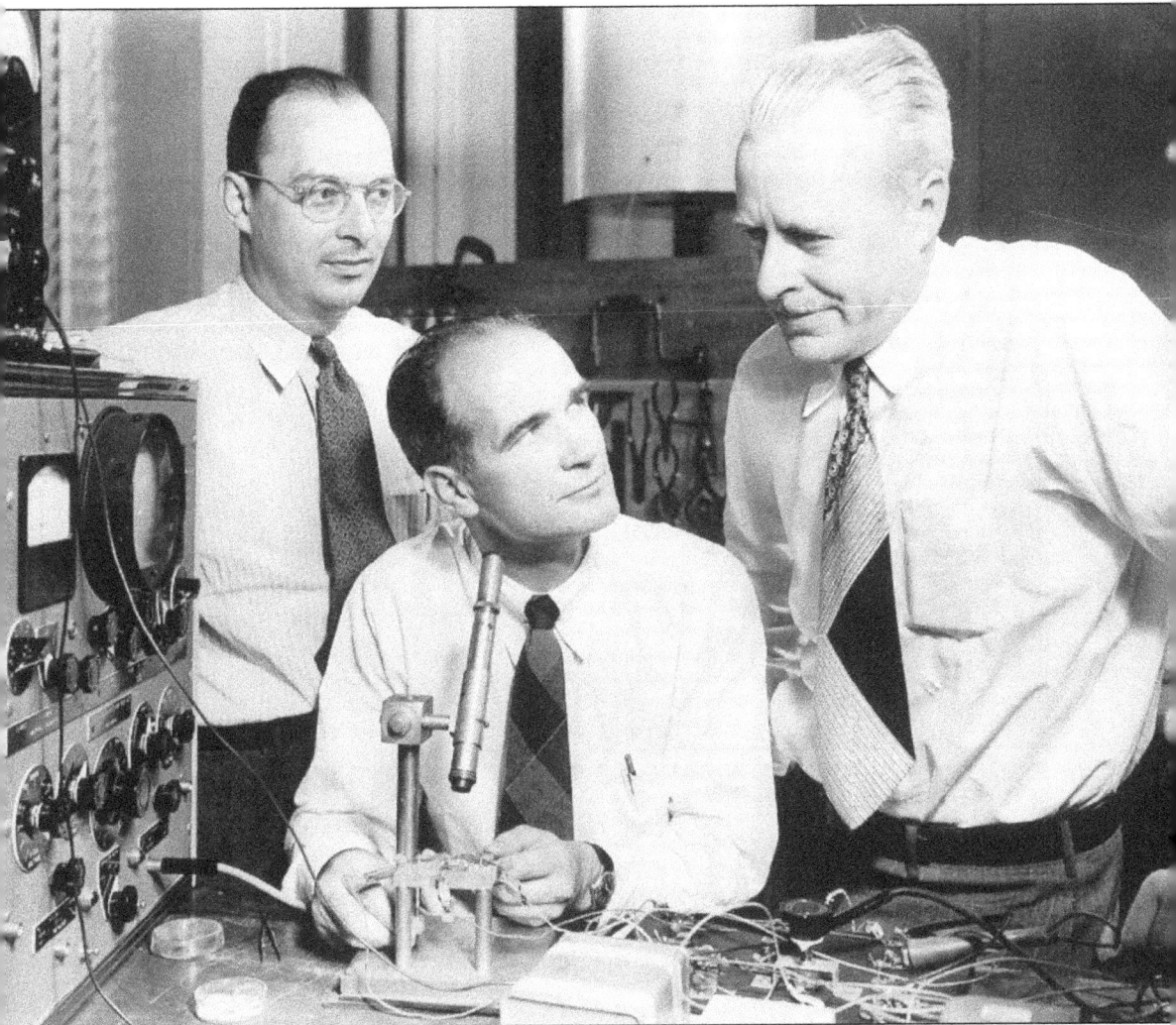

INVENTORS OF THE TRANSISTOR. Doctors John Bardeen (left), William Shockley, and Walter H. Brattain display apparatus used in the first investigations that led to their invention of the transistor at Bell Labs in Murray Hill in 1948. In 1956 they shared the Alfred B. Nobel Prize for Physics. With its small size, low operating current, and low cost, the transistor quickly displaced the vacuum tube in electronic devices and has been one of the most significant scientific discoveries of the twentieth century. The transistor ushered in an unprecedented revolution in telecommunications as well as bringing global changes to almost every area of human endeavor, including transportation, entertainment, medicine, education, and finance. (Property of AT&T Archives; Reprinted with permission of AT&T.)

SOLAR POWER TO SOLAR CELL. On April 25, 1954, Bell Labs demonstrated the first practical solar cell, a device that converts the sun's energy directly into useful amounts of electricity. Two Murray Hill scientists show that solar energy can power a radio transmitter. (Property of AT&T Archives; Reprinted with permission of AT&T.)

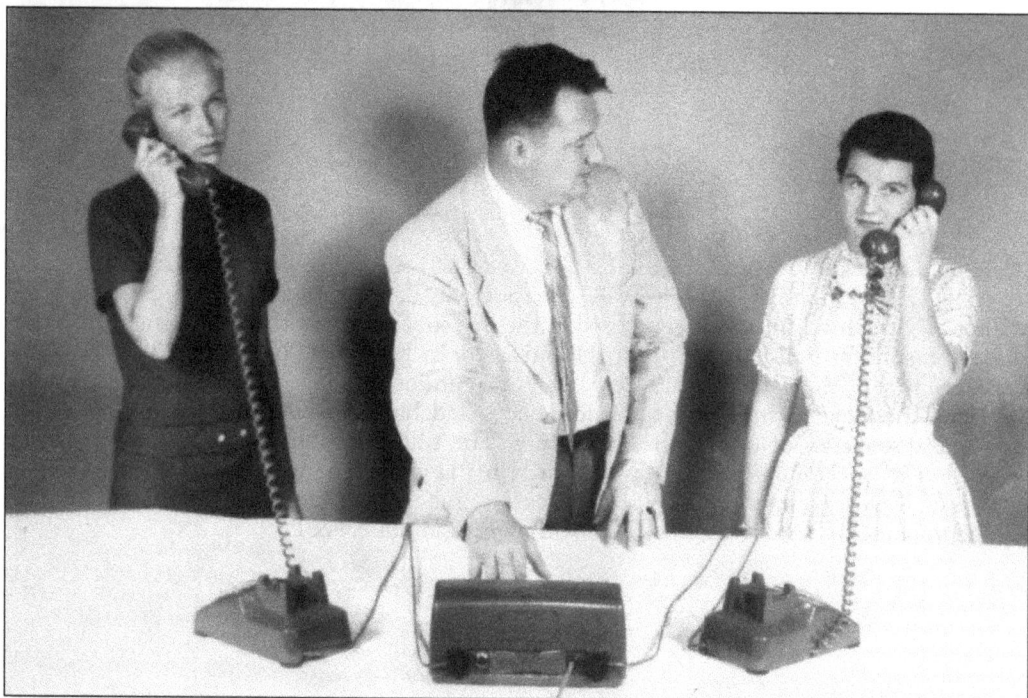

NUMBER PLEASE? Bell Labs employees Barbara Weiss (left), Walter Grote, and Mary Lou Landwehr demonstrate the operation of a teletrainer on July 22, 1958, in Murray Hill. (Mary Lou Weller.)

BLUE JAYS. This team was one of two softball teams in the Summit League fielded by Bell Labs in 1944. (Property of AT&T Archives; Reprinted with permission of AT&T.)

"LAST ONE IN IS . . . " Members of the Bell Labs swim club enjoyed swimming for fitness and fun and learned lifesaving skills at a local pool in 1945. (George Bebbington.)

SANTA'S WORKSHOP, 1946. Bell Labs employees Lois Burford (center) and Grace Murphy assist Santa Claus (a k a N.F. Marinaro) in setting up the Christmas toy collection booth in the Murray Hill lounge. (Property of AT&T Archives; Reprinted with permission of AT&T.)

HOLIDAY HAPPENING, c. 1949. Bell Labs employees leave the Arnold Auditorium in Murray Hill after a Christmas program. (Property of AT&T Archives; Reprinted with permission of AT&T.)

CHECKMATE! Murray Hill workers concentrate on their next moves during lunchtime chess games in 1946. (Property of AT&T Archives; Reprinted with permission of AT&T.)

UP, UP, AND AWAY! Bell Labs Model Airplane Club member E. Babcock Jr. flies his model plane from the Murray Hill lawn in September 1946 for a noontime crowd of spectators. (Property of AT&T Archives; Reprinted with permission from AT&T.)

ALL ABOARD!, c. 1950. Bell Labs' model railroad buffs keep their eyes on the tracks. (George Bebbington.)

WHO'S ON FIRST? This Murray Hill Labs all-star game was played in 1954. (George Bebbington.)

Four

Dramatis Personae

MAKING MUSIC, *c.* 1905. Walter Burgmiller, a descendant of Louis Burgmiller (who came to Berkeley Heights from Germany *c.* 1835), plays his guitar under a grape arbor at his home on Emerson Lane. *See also pages 95 and 101.* (Gail Shaffer.)

DAISY DAY, c. 1900. Daisy's portrait provides us with the lasting image of a dignified and demure turn-of-the-century teenager. Daisy and her family lived on Emerson Lane. (Berkeley Heights Historical Society.)

ALTHEA DAY, c. 1900. With her long curls, proper hair bow, dainty frock, and graceful basket of flowers, Althea's picture reflects a time when children were expected to be seen and not heard. (Berkeley Heights Historical Society.)

SISTER ACT, *c.* 1910. Displaying their highly fashionable "twin" dolls, the Hardy girls certainly had no immediate cause for sibling rivalry. The Hardy family was related to the Mercier-Burgmillers of Emerson Lane. (Berkeley Heights Historical Society.)

ALICE AND RUTH ROGERS, *c.* 1915. Alice and Ruth were descendants of Thomas Rogers, who arrived here in 1859 from New York and operated a huge farm covering parts of Berkeley Heights, Watchung, and Warren. The Rogers family called themselves the "First Irish on the Hill." (Berkeley Heights Historical Society.)

GRANDMOTHER KATHERINE, c. 1890. Born in Naples, Italy, Katherine was Peter Romano's mother and was the matriarch of the Romano family of Springfield Avenue. (Mary Lou Weller.)

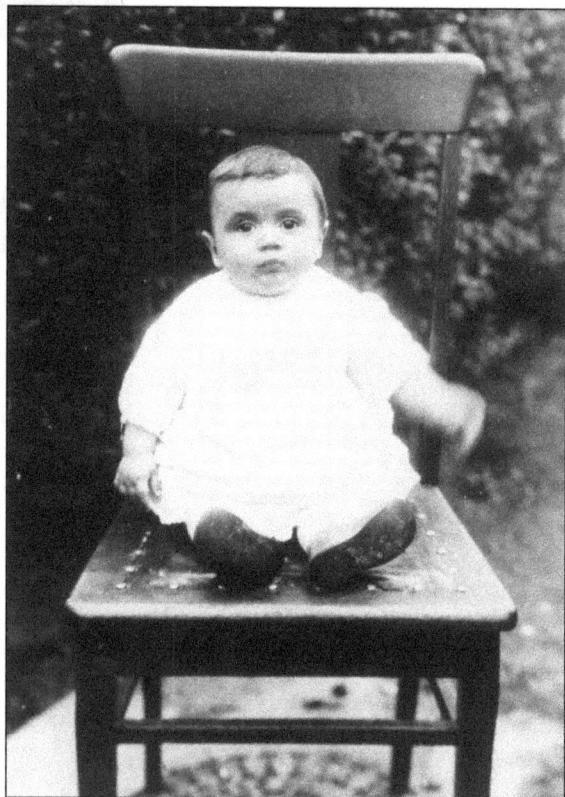

CARMEL ROMANO AT TWO YEARS OLD, c. 1923. The eleventh of Peter Romano's twelve children, Carmel takes her seat in a big, straight-backed chair with all the seriousness such an occasion demands. (Mary Lou Weller.)

WORLD WAR I ARMY BUDDIES. Mike Venezia (left) and Coney Delia joined the army together in 1917. They were stationed at Fort Dix, New Jersey, but were not shipped overseas because the war ended. (Anthony Delia.)

NAVY MEN, WORLD WAR II. Berkeley Heights friends Nelson Ahlquist (left) and Tommy Magliaro are home on leave c. 1942. Nelson was killed in action in the Pacific on the aircraft carrier Bunker Hill. (Ernie DeFronzo.)

"FROM THIS DAY FORWARD . . ." Coney Delia and his bride, Anna Triano Delia, were married in 1923 and settled in town to raise their family. *See also page 92.* (Anthony Delia.)

JOSEPH AND ROSE DEL DUCA,
c. 1900. Joseph Del Duca made his first
trip to America from Italy in 1893.
He later returned to his homeland to
bring his bride to Berkeley Heights
in 1896. Joseph and Rose had eight
children: Mary, Angelo, Rose,
Lucy, Josephine, Salvatore, Frances,
and Carmel. (Frances Truppi.)

MAN ABOUT TOWN. Born in 1905,
Salvatore Del Duca, son of Joseph and
Rose, served as the building inspector in
Berkeley Heights for forty years. His long
list of affiliations includes thirty years'
service as an active member of the fire
department and charter member status
in the rescue squad. Del Duca was also
a planning board member, builder, and
developer. (Frances Truppi.)

Mrs. Antonette Delia

request the honor of your presence at the
marriage of her daughter

Minnie C.

to

Mr. Michael A. Del Duca

on Wednesday morning, September 10, 1930, 10 o'clock

at the Little Flower Church
Berkeley Heights, N. J.

will be at home after Sept. 17
Washington St., Berkeley Heights, N. J.

DELIA WEDDING INVITATION.
(Angela Sampson.)

ALMOST THERE! Amid a porchful
of well-wishers, Miss Minnie Delia
pauses a moment at her home on
Springfield Avenue before leaving
for Little Flower Roman Catholic
Church to become Mrs. Michael
A. Del Duca. (Angela Sampson.)

FIRST COUPLE. Now husband and wife, Minnie Delia Del Duca and Michael A. Del Duca became the first couple to be married at the newly completed Little Flower Church on Plainfield Avenue. The wedding was celebrated with a nuptial high mass on September 10, 1930. Twenty-five years later, the couple's daughter, Angela, was married to Allan Sampson at Little Flower on the same day. (Angela Sampson.)

MINNIE AND MICHAEL'S RECEPTION. Wedding guests gather for a gala September afternoon reception outside the Delia home on Springfield Avenue. (Angela Sampson.)

HONEYMOON'S OVER! After their wedding trip to Rhode Island, Minnie and Michael Del Duca moved into their new home on Washington Street, which Michael had built for his bride. (Angela Sampson.)

IMAGE OF A FAMILY, c. 1920. Angelina and Jim Venezia of Springfield Avenue pose with their young daughter, Maria. (Ernie DeFronzo.)

MILDRED M. VENEZIA, 1929. The daughter of James and Maria Venezia, Mildred stands for her portrait as a bridesmaid at the wedding of her sister, Mary Venezia, to Ernest DeFronzo. Mildred later served as a Union County committeewoman for twenty-six years. (Ernie DeFronzo.)

CHURCH FOUNDER. Angelo J. Del Duca served as trustee of the Little Flower Roman Catholic Church from 1930 (when the church was organized) until 1973. The 50th anniversary booklet of the church describes him as "available day and night—when and wherever needed. He gave his heart to his work during the years he served as trustee . . ." (Nadine Tokash.)

63

THE DELIAS, *c.* 1905. Carmela and Antonio Delia pose with their daughters. From left to right are: (front row) Asia, Antonette, and Millie; (back row) Carmela (with Anna on her lap), Lucy, Mamie, and Antonio (with Tessie on his lap). The couple's sons and daughter Lena are not pictured. (Angela Sampson.)

"I TAKE THEE, ANGELA . . ." A.M. Del Duca and Angela Cardone Del Duca were married in the early 1900s and raised seven children in town. (Angela Sampson.)

GIDDYAP!, c. 1920. Joseph (on pony) and James Del Duca enjoy happy times with every child's dream—a real, live pony. Just a few years later, tragedy struck the Del Duca family when both brothers died in World War II within six months of each other. (Angela Sampson.)

LONG-TERM COMMITTEEMAN. In 1912 Angelo M. Del Duca, who was always called "A.M.," became a member of the township committee and, with the exception of three years, served continuously until 1950. He was also a member of the Elks Club, the Knights of Columbus, and the Mount Carmel Society. (Angela Sampson.)

MUSIC MAN, 1929. Ernest DeFronzo, the husband of Mary Venezia, strums his banjo on his front steps on Park Avenue. (Ernie DeFronzo.)

LET US ENTERTAIN YOU! The Berkeley Heights Ragtime Band with Walter Pedersen at the piano played for local banquets and parties during the 1950s. (Ernie DeFronzo.)

DOORWAY TO THE STARS. Dorothy Burgmiller Carr from Berkeley Heights was a pioneering airline stewardess in the early 1940s. Dorothy, whose husband was a pilot, stands at the door of a TWA Sky-Sleeper at United Airport in Burbank, California. In these early years, airline hostesses were required to be registered nurses as well as good-looking. A uniform like the one Dorothy is wearing is on display at the Smithsonian Air and Space Museum in Washington, D.C. (Gail Shaffer.)

LUCK OF THE DRAW, c. 1939. This group is engrossed in a game of gin rummy at the firehouse in the newly finished township complex on Park Avenue. From left to right are: A.M. Del Duca, Frank Petrone, Frank Vicendese Sr., Dominick Amodeo, and Michael Del Duca. (Angela Sampson.)

MEETING HAS COME TO ORDER, 1938. Berkeley Heights Township Committee members concentrate on civic matters. From left to right are: (seated) A.M. Del Duca, George W. Robbins Jr., Carl Radzio, Chairman A.C. Swenson, and H.M. Kent; (standing) Township Attorney John L. Hughes and Township Clerk William Russo. (Barnaby Kent.)

FIRST POLICEMAN, 1925. Chief D.V. Russo Jr. served as the first township policeman and is shown here on duty on Springfield Avenue near the Passaic River. For many years the New Jersey State Police maintained barracks on the corner of Springfield and Snyder Avenues where officers would stay for a week at a time to help keep law and order in Berkeley Heights and other small towns that had few police officers. (Bo Bosefskie.)

OUR FINEST. Members of the Berkeley Heights police force are ready to step out in the first township Memorial Day parade in May 1956. From left to right are: (front row) Harold Curtis (later police chief), Chief D.V. Russo Jr., and Captain Vito La Sasso; (middle row) George Sidor and A.F. Christensen (later traffic safety officer); (back row) Vito Amodeo, Donald Brian, and Ralph Del Duca (later police chief). (Bo Bosefskie.)

CHARLES S. HOAG, MOUNTED POLICEMAN, *c.* 1942. Well known for years as the special officer on the horse in the Watchung Reservation, Charles Hoag later became the Union County police chief. A native of Kansas, Chief Hoag made his home in the Deserted Village. He served with the county police for thirty-eight years, retiring in 1980. He died in the early 1990s. (Bo Bosefskie.)

FIREFIGHTERS' FIRST PHOTO, July 16, 1930. Members of the Berkeley Heights Volunteer Fire Company Number One are, from left to right: (front row) August Montasano, Anthony Petrone, Foreman Carl Carpenter, Michael Del Duca, Chief John Amodeo, Salvatore Del Duca, Nicholas Monica, Coney Delia, and Angelo J. Del Duca; (middle row) Anthony Amiano, Frank Uzzolino, Assistant Foreman Xavier Masterson, Ernest Radzio, Michael Amodeo, Official Chaplain Father Matthew J. Toohey, Charles La Sasso, Anthony DeBisco, Ross Iannello, and Joseph Mondelli; (back row) Driver Dominick Imbimbo and John Sperenzi. Behind the group is a 600-gallon-per-minute pumper equipped with 1,000 feet of 2.5-inch fire hose, 12 pairs of boots, 12 raincoats, 2 nozzles, a 28-foot extension ladder, and a hand siren. (Bo Bosefskie.)

ALWAYS ON CALL, c. 1952. The Berkeley Heights Rescue Squad answered its first call on January 11, 1943. From left to right are: (front row) Captain Floyd Fredericks, Robert Andrus, Salvatore Del Duca, Mayor A.C. Swenson, Hazel Corby, unidentified, Mildred Shaffer, Xavier Masterson, and Barnaby Kent; (back row) two unidentified members, G.H. Crockett, Robert Del Duca, George Vanderoef, Gil Bischoff, and George Galla. (Bo Bosefskie.)

RESCUE SQUAD PRESENTATION, 1961. Squad President Walter Bower (second from left) presents a commemorative plaque to Captain Edward Damanski honoring his dedicated service to the squad. Standing by are members Bob Young, Gail Shaffer, and Jerry Rickleffs. The rescue squad building on Locust Avenue was dedicated in 1960. (Berkeley Heights Rescue Squad.)

Five

Villages Within

FELTVILLE MILL, c. 1929. New York stationery manufacturer David Felt chose the Blue Brook Valley between the first and second Watchung Mountains in what is now Berkeley Heights for his paper mill community (1845–1860). He purchased about 760 acres with two existing mills and built this mill, which was torn down in 1930. (Berkeley Heights Historical Society.)

FELTVILLE, 1845–1860. This c. 1964 drawing by Mr. and Mrs. Walter J. Young depicts a thriving but isolated village which must have fulfilled David Felt's vision of a complete community for his workers away from the dangers and temptations of city life. About two hundred people lived here during Feltville's prosperous years. Mr. Felt sold the entire complex in 1860 and returned to New York City. Other entrepreneurs tried six different enterprises on the property, but their ultimate failure led to the name Deserted Village. In 1882 Warren Ackerman of Scotch Plains

took ownership of the land and opened a family resort here called Glenside Park. Although it prospered for a number of years, the advent of the automobile provided vacationers with other choices and by 1916, the summer retreat closed and the village was deserted once more. The entire Deserted Village is listed on both the State and the National Registers of Historic Places. (New Providence Historical Society, Trailside Museum Association.)

FELTVILLE CHURCH AND STORE, c. 1906. David Felt provided for all the needs of his employees; there was a church on the second floor of this building and a general store downstairs. The belfry was added later. "King David," as Mr. Felt was often called, summoned his workers to their daily tasks, to church on Sundays, and to a nightly 9 pm curfew with the ringing of a loud bell. (New Providence Historical Society, Trailside Museum Association.)

MILL HANDS' COTTAGE, REAR VIEW, c. 1900. David Felt's workers lived in two-family houses such as this one pictured during the Glenside Park era. The cottages had two front and two back doors during Mr. Felt's time, but the porches were later additions. David Felt also established a post office at Feltville, one of fourteen post offices at that time in Essex County, which included Union County until 1857. (Berkeley Heights Historical Society.)

FELTVILLE SCHOOL, *c.* 1890. David Felt built a school (the porch was a later addition), a blacksmith shop, and other buildings. His Stationers' Hall Press produced stationery, business journals, printed pamphlets, and books. Only one volume, John Littell's 1852 *Genealogies*, is known to exist today. At the time of this photograph the school was serving as the Glenside Park gatehouse. (Berkeley Heights Historical Society.)

GLENSIDE PARK COTTAGES, *c.* 1891. Six and ten-room cottages such as these were rented for the season for $100 to $250, completely furnished except for linens. Glenside also featured electric lights on the roads and spacious grounds for golf, tennis, croquet, and baseball. (Cranford Historical Society.)

GLENSIDE PARK FESTIVITIES, c. 1891. These young ladies wearing garlands of flowers may be awaiting a May Day celebration at Glenside Park. A brochure advertising Glenside Park emphasized the good train service to New York from the Murray Hill station. Arriving guests could arrange carriage transportation to the resort for 50¢ per person. (Cranford Historical Society.)

RADDER FAMILY, c. 1938. This family, shown here standing on Glenside Avenue, lived in the Feltville schoolhouse (left) for several years. Despite its failures, the Deserted Village is alive and well today. The Union County Division of Parks and Recreation is involved in a stabilization and restoration project of the ten existing structures and teaches archaeological techniques to schoolchildren through simulated digs on the property. (New Providence Historical Society, Trailside Museum Association.)

SEELEY'S MILL, c. 1916. Located on Green Brook in Scotch Plains, Seeley's Mill was part of Edmund A. Seeley's paper mill company, a thriving business until 1924. Originally built in 1763 and called Fall Mill, the gristmill was vital to early settlers of Berkeley Heights for grinding grains. This view shows Seeley's Mill collapsing into Green Brook after a torrential storm caused rampaging flood waters. (Berkeley Heights Historical Society.)

ENTRANCE TO FREE ACRES, c. 1920. This unique, single-tax village founded in 1910 by Bolton Hall, a New York lawyer and Emerson Lane property owner, continues today as a vibrant, vital community. Free Acres is located in the southwestern corner of the township with a small area in Watchung. Mr. Hall may have named Emerson Lane for Ralph Waldo Emerson, the American essayist and poet. (Gail Shaffer.)

FREE ACRES FOUNDER, c. 1920. Bolton Hall was influenced by the ideas of American writer, economist, and reformer Henry George (1835–1897) and founded Free Acres to put George's premise, known as the single-tax theory, into practice. Free Acres began as a summer retreat for artistic city residents of moderate means and evolved into a year-round community. The land belonged to the community as a whole with residents paying rent to the Free Acres Association, who in turn paid real estate taxes to the township in a lump sum. Although changes have occurred, Free Acres still functions within a single-tax framework. Its eighty-five families remain committed to preserving its narrow, gently curving roads, historic red farmhouse, hidden gardens, old trees, and meandering brook. (Berkeley Heights Historical Society.)

FREE ACREITES, c. 1920. Two beloved early residents of Free Acres were Anna Elizabeth Johnson and her husband, William C. Johnson, who was affectionately known as "Pop." (Berkeley Heights Historical Society.)

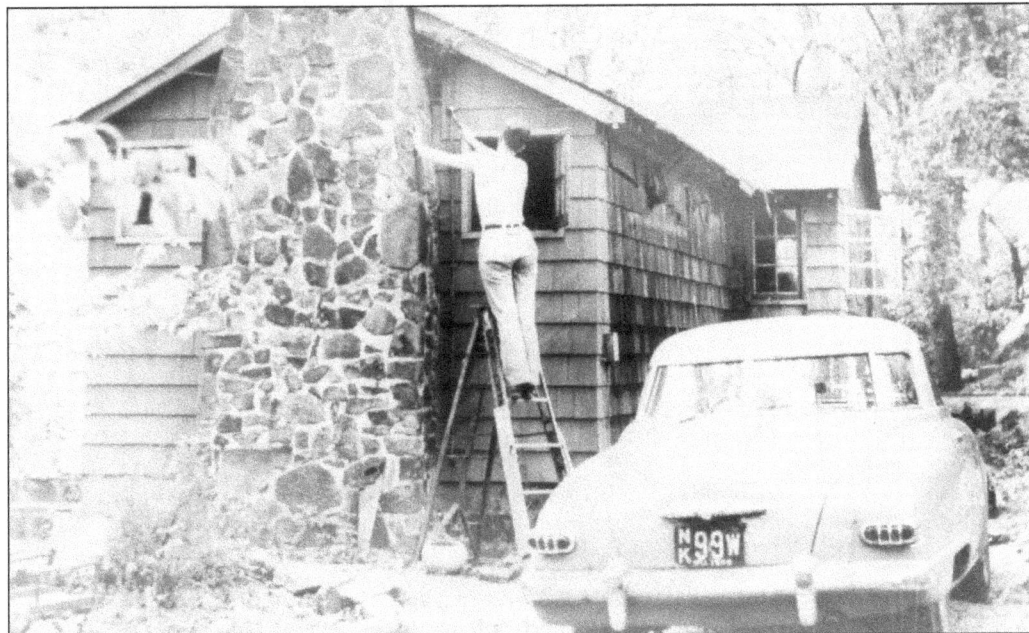

HOME OF THE CLAY FAMILY, 1949. In 1920, Katharine Clay and her family moved to Free Acres, where the five Clay children grew up. One of her sons is shown here making repairs to their house and its imposing stone chimney. Katharine's daughter, Katharine (Kay) Clay Williams, still lives in Berkeley Heights. *See also page 86.* (Newark Public Library.)

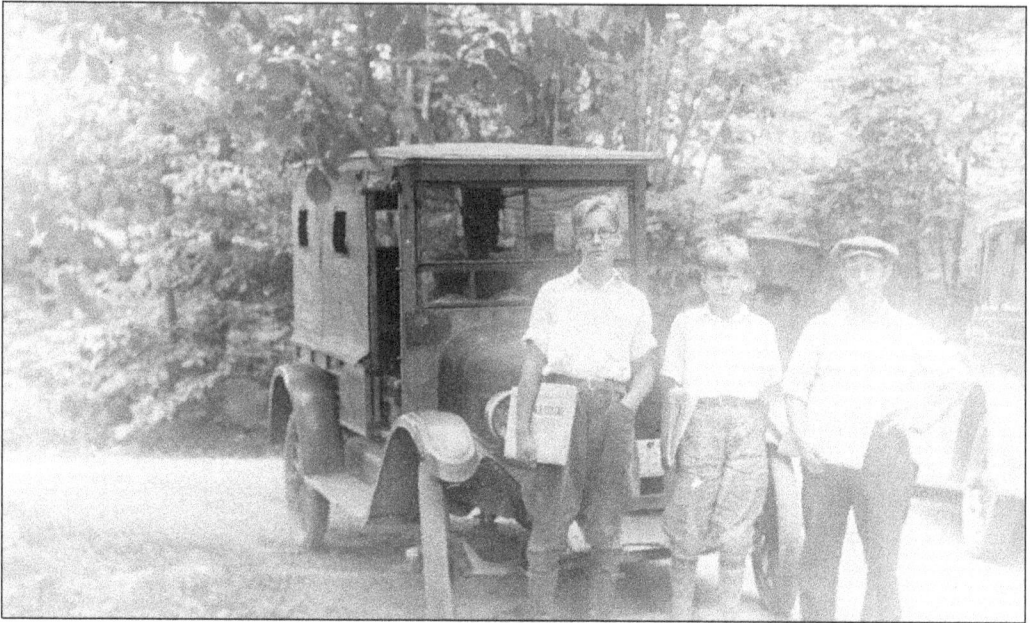

FREE ACRES NEWSBOYS, c. 1920. Local lads stop for a snapshot as they make their appointed rounds. Notice the high-laced boots and knickers worn by the boys, who must have felt very much in step with the times. (Berkeley Heights Historical Society.)

WILL CRAWFORD, c. 1920. Illustrator and staff artist for several New York newspapers, "Uncle Bill" was an integral part of the Free Acres community from 1915 until his death in 1944. He served as the town forester and designed posters, puppets, costumes, and his highly original carved wood signs. The sign pictured here was carved for the archery guild, the Locksley Archers. (Berkeley Heights Historical Society.)

LOCKSLEY ARCHERS, c. 1920. Organized by Will Crawford (far right), the Locksley Archers often dressed in Robin Hood costumes for tournaments and other special events. On the far left is Thorne Smith, author of the witty, gently satiric *Topper* books. His wife, Celia Sullivan Smith, is second from the right. When writing *Topper*, Smith was influenced by the ambiance of Free Acres and by individual residents. Cosmo Topper, a banker and New Jersey suburbanite, finds his predictable life drastically changed when he is suddenly thrown into a world of zany ghosts. *Topper* was the most popular of Mr. Smith's novels, and in 1937 it was made into a movie featuring Cary Grant, Constance Bennett, and Roland Young. Other movies and a television series followed. (Berkeley Heights Historical Society.)

THE BROWNS, 1960. Lizbeth Undena "Betty" Brown and her husband, Edmund Livingston Brown, were longtime Free Acres residents known for their love of and concern for nature. In 1960, Sidney Beinfest, also of Free Acres, undertook the project of photographing all those living in the community at that time. (Sidney Beinfest, Free Acres Archives.)

THE BRODNEYS, 1960. Edith and Spencer Brodney were another well-known Free Acres couple. Mrs. Brodney was a nursery school teacher, while her husband was an editor of the *New York Times* and a political magazine known as *Events*. (Sidney Beinfest, Free Acres Archives.)

WHEN KNIGHTS WERE BOLD, 1948. The Moldenke Castle, just across the Berkeley Heights border in Watchung, must have seemed like a fairy tale come true for Free Acres children who hiked through the woods to peer at this remarkable replica of a German castle on the Rhine. Built in 1900 by the cast-iron metallurgist Dr. Richard Moldenke, the castle was demolished about 1970. (Newark Public Library.)

END OF SUMMER PARTY, 1950. The Free Acres community, many in costume, gathers outside the farmhouse to celebrate the changing seasons. Many of the children pictured here later purchased homes of their own in Free Acres, thus imparting the heritage and traditions of this unique place to the next generation. (Free Acres Archives.)

FREE ACRES' TOWN MEETING, 1960. Town Clerk Katharine Clay and Harry Goldman chair an August meeting of the Free Acres Association. Residents continue to meet monthly to address concerns and make decisions for the community. (Sidney Beinfest, Free Acres Archives.)

FREE ACRES' BLACKBOARD, 1960. For many years the blackboard was used at Free Acres town meetings for electing members to the association's various committees, such as health and sanitation and roads and survey. (Sidney Beinfest, Free Acres Archives.)

Six

"Merrily We Roll Along"

MOVIN' DAY IN THE TOWNSHIP, *c.* 1890. The faithful horse and wagon might be slow, especially when hauling heavy household goods, but they were still an affordable form of transportation by the end of the nineteenth century. (Rita Ragno.)

JEANNETTE BURGMILLER, c. 1915. Jeannette's patient horse awaits her next command. A member of the Mercier-Burgmiller family, Jeannette lived on Emerson Lane. The arrival of the railroad in Berkeley Heights made it possible for her to commute to New York City for her job as a bookkeeper. Her twin sister Agnes, an alumna of Barnard College, taught at Columbia School. (Gail Shaffer.)

DOWN HOME, c. 1900. This unidentified, local family seated on their farm wagon typifies the rural character of Berkeley Heights which lasted well into the twentieth century. (Berkeley Heights Historical Society.)

PROUD CAR OWNER, *c.* 1920. John Couser, the first Bonnie Burn Sanatorium groundskeeper, was one of many Americans who purchased Henry Ford's mass-produced, reliable "Model T." John Couser married Gladys Rogers, daughter of early settler Thomas Rogers. (Newark Public Library.)

NEW MODES, OLD MODES, 1915. The Burgmiller girls of Emerson Lane pose in a newfangled, horseless carriage alongside an ancient source of water, the well. (Gail Shaffer.)

"THE HORSE KNOWS THE WAY," c. 1890. Crane-Day family members of Springfield Avenue appear ready to trot off to church or a Sunday afternoon buggy ride. (Berkeley Heights Historical Society.)

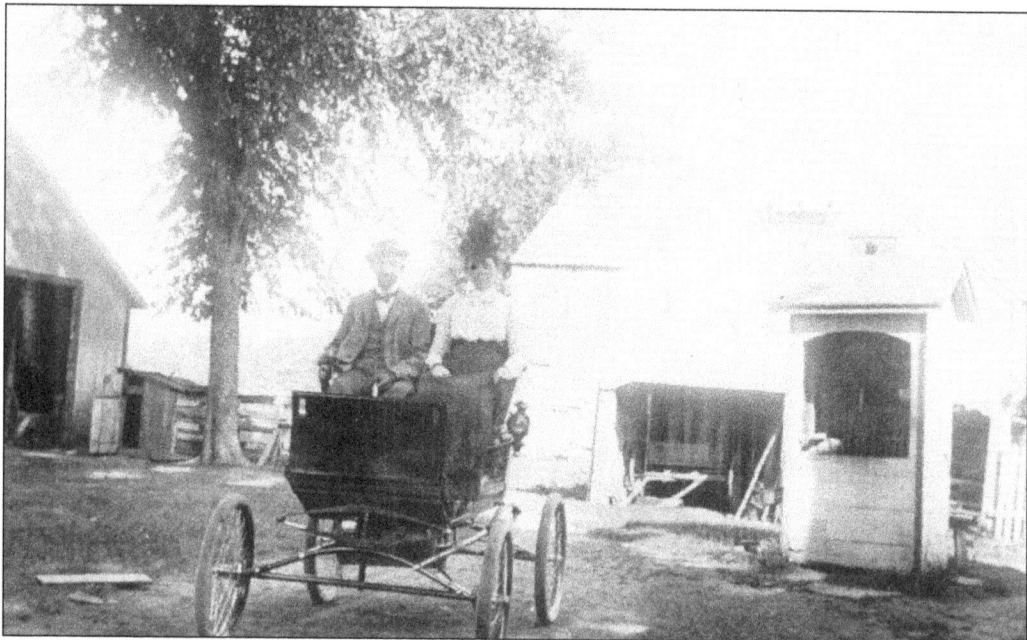

STEPHEN AND HATTIE DAY, c. 1910. Heads must have turned along the narrow, dusty roads of Berkeley Heights when this couple chugged by in their stylish locomobile. (Berkeley Heights Historical Society.)

REUNION, *c.* 1905. Crane-Day relatives at the Murray Hill railroad station are probably awaiting rides to attend their family gathering in Berkeley Heights. The Crane-Day extended family must have comprised a large group of all ages by this time, more than a century after the pioneering Joseph Crane first bought land on Springfield Avenue. (Berkeley Heights Historical Society.)

ARE WE THERE YET?, *c.* 1905. Some of the Crane-Day kinsfolk arriving at the Springfield Avenue homestead take advantage of a family automobile for a photograph opportunity. (Rita Ragno.)

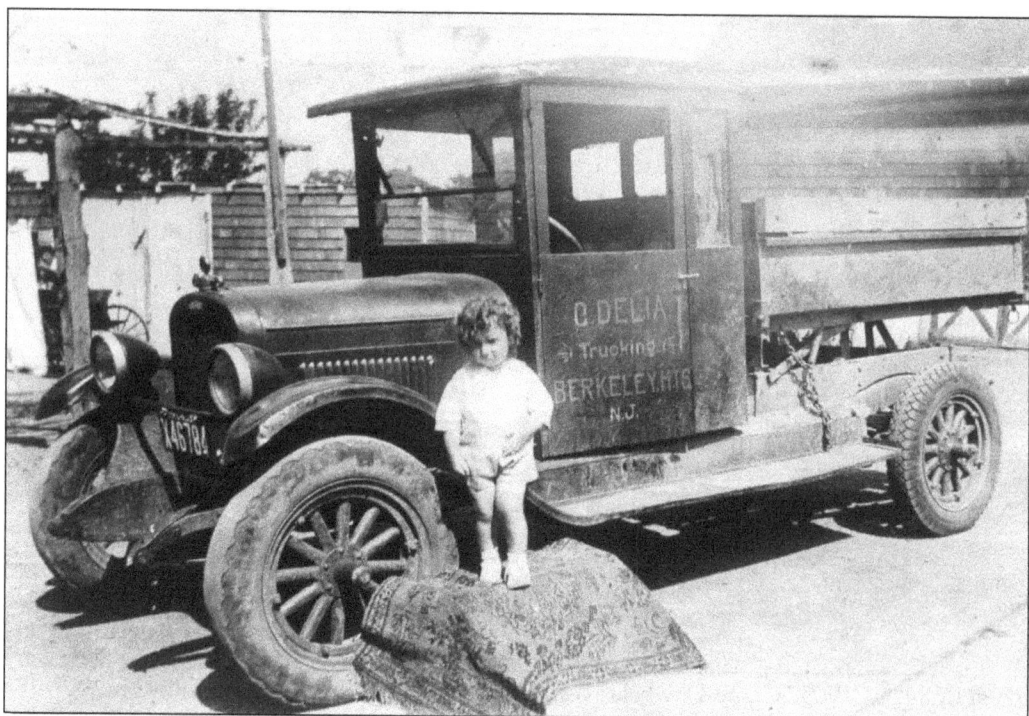

SAM DELIA AND DAD'S FIRST TRUCK, early 1930s. A slightly shy, eighteen-month-old Sam stands on a special, carpeted step stool beside Coney Delia's International truck, parked at the family farm on Garfield Street and Summit Avenue. (Bo Bosefskie.)

CONEY AND ANTHONY DELIA, c. 1933. With his father in the driver's seat, Sam's brother Anthony poses on the running board of a new International truck. The old truck is parked to the left. Coney Delia maintained a trucking and landscaping business along with his family farm. (Anthony Delia.)

"GENTLEMAN, START YOUR ENGINE!" Venezia family members are ready and waiting to motor around the countryside. (Berkeley Heights Historical Society.)

NEW PROVIDENCE TOWNSHIP, 1872. This detail, possibly from a *New Jersey State Atlas* map, indicates the route of the New Jersey West Line Railroad through the area. The Ellendor Station (center left), located at Snyder Avenue, was abandoned about 1888 when well-to-do resident Cornelius Runkle built the existing Plainfield Avenue station. Another early businessman, W.A. Ostrander, presumably named the Ellendor station for his wife. (Rita Ragno.)

STEAM TRAIN, 1920. A steam locomotive pulling passenger cars on the Delaware, Lackawanna, and Western Railroad, familiarly known as the "Delay, Linger, and Wait," chugs into the Berkeley Heights railroad station. Easily the most recognized and beloved of all Berkeley Heights landmarks, the railroad station still remains in its original condition, although it is painted yellow now, instead of red. (Rita Ragno.)

END OF THE LINE, 1930. The last steam train heading toward Berkeley Heights from Summit approaches the spot where Snyder Avenue would later cross the railroad tracks. Looking toward the northeast, the township was still quite undeveloped at this time with no houses in sight. Note the overhead power wire for the new electric trains. (Carol Drake Friedman.)

94

DOWN BY THE STATION, 1930. Crowds await the arrival of the first Delaware, Lackawanna, and Western (later the Erie Lackawanna and now New Jersey Transit) electric train to stop at the Berkeley Heights railroad station. Flags flew and children were excused from school for this momentous occasion. (Carol Drake Friedman.)

TAXI!, c. 1920. Transportation to and from the railroad station was in the capable hands of Walter Burgmiller (center, next to the cab), first with a horse and wagon, and then with his taxi. The station was built in the popular Stick style of the late nineteenth century, a style which displays its framing timbers on the exterior of the building. (Gail Shaffer.)

RIDE A WRECK, 1929. Even an old Ford flivver without tires was fun to climb aboard, as attested to by these young Venezia family members. (Ernie DeFronzo.)

DOWN THE SHORE, c. 1950. Berkeley Heights boys pause for a snapshot on their way to the beach at Point Pleasant. From left to right are: (front row) Jim Delia, Sam Delia (seated), Joe Cerulli (seated on fender), and Anton Delia; (back row) Mike Mazzarisi and Jim Vicendese. (Bo Bosefskie.)

Seven

Back to School

DIAMOND HILL SCHOOL, c. 1932. Children in grades one through eight attended this school on Diamond Hill Road, also known as the Woodchuck School. It closed in 1934, the last one-room schoolhouse in Union County to shut its doors. Built in 1888, the school building remains on its original foundation and continues as a private home. (Bo Bosefskie.)

OLD BRICK SCHOOL, c. 1910. Early educators William Woodruff (top left) and Agnes Burgmiller (top right) stand with students at the Old Brick School, now part of an apartment building on Plainfield Avenue. Students attended classes here until the first floor of Columbia School was finished in 1912. (Berkeley Heights Historical Society.)

COLUMBIA SCHOOL, c. 1915. Built in the Romanesque Revival style often used for schools, churches, and other public buildings at that time, Columbia School's huge doorway arch remains an impressive example of this architectural tradition. When the school was enlarged in later years, this section became home to the board of education and administrative offices. The rest of the building now houses the Columbia Middle School. (Rita Ragno.)

COLUMBIA SCHOOL GRADUATES, 1922. Mildred Burgmiller Shaffer and Kenneth Berkeley Shaffer were members of one of the first eighth grade graduating classes at Columbia School. Mildred later became Kenneth's sister-in-law when she married his brother, Frank Clifford Shaffer Jr. Their daughter, Gail Shaffer, a lifelong resident of Berkeley Heights, has been a teacher at the Governor Livingston Regional High School for many years. And, yes, Kenneth's middle name does represent the town he was born in, Berkeley Heights! (Gail Shaffer.)

COLUMBIA SCHOOL, *c.* 1913. Students stand with their teacher, Olive Bogert of Gillette, beneath the arch at the front door of the new school for grades one through eight on Plainfield Avenue. (Berkeley Heights Historical Society.)

COLUMBIA SCHOOL EIGHTH GRADE GRADUATING CLASS, *c.* 1923. Many students did not go to high school after graduating from the eighth grade but went to work on their family farms or in local businesses. Students who continued their schooling attended Summit High School until the Jonathan Dayton Regional High School in Springfield opened in the 1930s. (Gail Shaffer.)

COLUMBIA SCHOOL FACULTY, 1936. Supervising Principal William Woodruff is pictured here at the time of his retirement. From left to right are: (front row) Miss Fenn (later Mrs. Stilwell), Miss Deinlein, Miss Pringle, Mr. Woodruff, Miss Sayre, Miss Labo, and Miss Bost (later Mrs. Del Duca); (back row) Miss Stadley, Miss Marguerite Stewart (later Mrs. Woods), Miss French (music teacher), and Miss Johnson (art teacher). (Berkeley Heights Historical Society.)

DON'T MISS THE BUS!, c. 1950. Walter Burgmiller, who earlier operated the town taxi, owned this township school bus and another one that he nicknamed "The Cheese Crate" because of its unusual shape. (Gail Shaffer.)

County School Certificate

State of  New Jersey

This Certifies that

Edna Sarah Kuntz

has satisfactorily completed the Course of Study prescribed for the Eighth Grade in this County and is therefore entitled to receive this

Certificate of Promotion

Given at Columbia School County of Union this fifteenth day of June 19 38

N. L. Johnson
County Superintendent of Schools

Eugene L. Miller
Supervising Officer

Principal

COLUMBIA SCHOOL DIPLOMA, 1938. (Bo Bosefskie.)

LITTLE FLOWER PARISH SCHOOL
Fund Drive
Sunday · Jan 29, 1961

GOAL $250,000

LITTLE FLOWER SCHOOL FUND DRIVE, 1961. After a successful building fund drive, the Little Flower Parish School opened in Berkeley Heights in September 1963 with 162 students in grades one through four. Each year another grade was added until all eight grades were in session. The first graduation was held in June 1968. In 1988 the Little Flower School was closed. (Little Flower Roman Catholic Church.)

Eight

All Around Town

IT'S TWINS! These calves born in the late 1930s on Coney Delia's farm on Garfield Street and Summit Avenue may have set a record as the only bovine twins born in New Jersey. Mr. Delia received the twins' mother from a Meyersville man in the logging business as part of a trade for two oak trees on the Delia property. Everyone involved was surprised to find out that the cow was pregnant with two calves! (Bo Bosefskie.)

LUCAS HOUSE, 1913. A New York City native and vice president of the Diamond Match Company, Henry G. (Harry) Lucas fondly remembered his childhood vacations in the area and bought a small house with a center chimney in Berkeley Heights in 1905. His home originally stood on several acres of land at Mountain and Plainfield Avenues, near where the Westminster Presbyterian Church is now located. (Rita Ragno.)

LUCAS HOUSE, 1920. Harry Lucas enlarged the second floor of his home with an extension over the front porch, transforming his settler's cottage into a suburban residence. His property was known as Lucas Corners. (Rita Ragno.)

LUCAS HOUSE, 1931. During this year Harry Lucas had his house moved 80 feet west because of road changes at Mountain and Plainfield Avenues. He enclosed the porch and added a handsome stone chimney and fireplace. He also personalized his home by placing a wrought iron "L" at the top of the chimney, which can be seen on the house to this day. (Rita Ragno.)

Taxes for 1907

Are now due and hereby demanded. If not paid to me before the 20th day of December next, the delinquents will be proceeded against according to law. Legal costs and interest at one per cent. per month will be added.

The sum to be raised on each $100 is:

State and County,	- - $ .44
Township and Poor	- - .20
Road,	- - - - - .32
Special Road,	- - - .04
Township School Tax,	- .56
Total,	- - - $1.56

Any taxpayer feeling aggrieved by the assessed valuation of his property may appeal to the Union County Board of Taxation, Elizabeth, N. J., filing with such board a petition setting forth nature and location of such assessed property, cause of complaint, and the relief sought.

Taxes will be received at my residence on all working days, in business hours, till December 20th, inclusive.

Township of New Providence, N. J., October 1st, 1907.

To...... Harry S. Lucas......

The valuation of your Taxable Property and your Assessment for Taxes in the Township of New Providence for the year 1907, are as follows:

	$	Cts.		$	Cts.
Number of Acres, . .	4 7/8				
Value of Real Estate, ...	400				
Value of Personal Estate, . .					
Amount of Levy, ...	400				
State and County Tax, ...				1	76
Township and Poor Tax, ...					80
Road Tax, ...				1	28
Interest on County Road Bonds, ...					16
School Tax, ...				2	24
Poll Tax, ...					
Dog Tax, ...					
TOTAL TAX, ...				6	24
Interest, ...					
Costs, ...					
Total Amount Due, ...					

LUCAS TAX BILL, 1907. No record has been found of Harry Lucas' feelings about his property tax charges, but by today's standards, he certainly had no cause for complaint! (Bo Bosefskie.)

HENRY G. LUCAS, 1916. An active township citizen, Harry Lucas was a member of the township committee, the board of education, the early fire companies, and a founder of the rescue squad. After he died in 1960, his second wife, Sarah Bohm Lucas, sold 5 acres of Lucas Corners to the Presbytery of Morris and Orange to build the Westminster Presbyterian Church on the corner of Mountain and Plainfield Avenues. (Berkeley Heights Historical Society.)

LITTLE HOUSE IN THE BACKYARD, c. 1910. This outhouse in a rustic setting on the corner of Mountain and Yale Avenues reminds us of that almost-forgotten mainstay of every household before the advent of indoor plumbing. (Rita Ragno.)

POST OFFICE, *c.* 1885. Hannah Wahl, perhaps standing at center behind the fence, served as the township postmistress from 1885 to 1900, maintaining the post office on the enclosed front porch of her home, now part of the Mondelli property on Plainfield Avenue. Hannah's husband, George, was a member of the township committee in the early 1900s. (Newark Public Library.)

HOME OF THE WAHLS, *c.* 1885. A more distant view of the home of Postmistress Hannah Wahl and her husband, George, reveals a busy Plainfield Avenue farm and home. It looks as though the Wahls were growing hops on their front arbor. (Berkeley Heights Historical Society.)

UNION VILLAGE METHODIST CHURCH, *c.* 1940. In 1798 settlers founded the Methodist Episcopal Church in New Providence. Some years later, the Berkeley Heights members and others organized a smaller group in Union Village at the crossroads from Watchung and Mount Bethel (Warren) to Gillette and New Providence. By 1825, the Union Village Methodists had grown in number, and on December 18 of that year they dedicated a new meetinghouse, sometimes called the "Little Church by the Wayside." In 1911, Henry S. Fullerton purchased a bell for the Union Village Church. When a new sanctuary was built in 1961, the bell was moved to the new belfry. For several years this old building was leased to the Stony Hill Players, and it was eventually sold as a residence. (Mary Lou Weller.)

MARY LOU AND BILL, 1960. Engaged couple Mary Lou Landwehr and Bill Weller stand on the steps of the original Union Village Methodist Church. They were married on February 18, 1961, at a candlelight ceremony at the old sanctuary, the next-to-last couple to celebrate their wedding there. Mary Lou Weller is a descendant of the Romano family, who settled on Springfield Avenue. (Mary Lou Weller.)

PROCESSION, 1955. Union Village Methodists make their way along Mountain Avenue from the church to the opening of their new educational building located just over the Berkeley Heights border in Warren. Many township residents are active in the Union Village Methodist Church to this day. (Mary Lou Weller.)

TIME FOR A SONG, c. 1905. Friends and family gather on the porch of the Shaffer home on Plainfield Avenue. John Wesley is standing. Frank Clifford Shaffer Sr., wearing a bow tie, is seated; his wife, Janet McLean Shaffer, is next to him. The child with the banjo is Frank Clifford Shaffer Jr., who was always called Clifford. This house was built in the 1750s and remains an attractive residence. (Rita Ragno.)

GROCERY STORE, c. 1930. Cousins and proprietors Raymond Rogers (left) and Clifford Shaffer relax on the front porch of their store on the corner of Plainfield Avenue and Rogers Place. Probably their most well-known customer was actor James Cagney, who shopped at the store while vacationing at Free Acres. In later years, O'Connor's Market was located here, and a professional building is currently on the site. (Gail Shaffer.)

BURGMILLER FARMHOUSE, c. 1910. Louis Burgmiller, who settled in the township c. 1830, married Louisa Mercier from an early French family. Their nine children remained in Berkeley Heights and were active in the community. From left to right are: (front row) Ruth Rogers and Lillian Stoats; (back row) Jeannette Burgmiller, Louise Burgmiller, Pauline Wahl, Agnes Burgmiller, and Ethel Wahl. (Gail Shaffer.)

COUSINS ALL AROUND, c. 1912. Two generations of Merciers, Burgmillers, and Simmonses assemble beside a pond located in a cow pasture off Emerson Lane. (Gail Shaffer.)

PUBLIC LIBRARY, 1924. Realtor William Jeffery could be called the first librarian in Berkeley Heights. In the early 1900s he stocked his office, this quaint building on the corner of Plainfield and Putnam Avenues, with books and left it open for commuters and other townsfolk to stop in and read. The Free Acres Association also organized a literary guild to circulate books and sponsor book talks. (Berkeley Heights Historical Society.)

MOUNT CARMEL HALL, c. 1930. Home of the Berkeley Heights Public Library since 1953, the original Mount Carmel Hall also served as the first Catholic church within Berkeley Heights. The first mass was celebrated on Christmas Day, 1926. Services continued at the hall until the Little Flower Church next door was completed in 1930. (Little Flower Roman Catholic Church.)

FREY HOME, c. 1928. The Frey family manufactured pottery and brick on Snyder Avenue, where clay was plentiful. Edward J. Frey Sr. stands at left and Edward J. Frey Jr. is kneeling at left. Other family members include Elizabeth, Mary, Nettie, Teresa, grandchild Edna, and Leonie Frey (Mrs. E.J. Sr.). Part of this house was built c. 1903, with an addition added later. (Carol Drake Friedman.)

WOODLAND POTTERY BUILDINGS, c. 1926. Owned by the Frey family, this company on Snyder Avenue produced vases, pitchers, jugs, and lamp bases that were sold at Lord and Taylor's in New York and other stores here and abroad. Woodland Pottery ceased operations in 1931. At the time of this picture, Snyder Avenue ended at the factory. It remained a dirt road for many years. (Carol Drake Friedman.)

OLD SAINT MARY'S STONY HILL, c. 1905. Saint Mary's Stony Hill Roman Catholic Church, located in Watchung at the Berkeley Heights border, was founded in 1847 by early German settlers from the township and the surrounding area. Strolling along Plainfield Avenue from the church are, from left to right: Mrs. McGoldrick, Agnes Burgmiller, unidentified, Charlotte Burgmiller, and Jeannette Burgmiller. (Gail Shaffer.)

OLD SAINT MARY'S STONY HILL POSTCARD, c. 1915. The parishioners outgrew their original 1847 church and laid the cornerstone for this second sanctuary on May 10, 1877. Many of the beams from the first building were incorporated into this larger, brick church. Services were held here until shortly before this beloved landmark was demolished in 1974. The name of Saint Mary's Stony Hill was transferred to a new church in Watchung. (Gail Shaffer.)

OLD SAINT MARY'S CENTENNIAL MASS. On July 16, 1954, the congregation of Saint Mary's Stony Hill Roman Catholic Church celebrated their 100th anniversary. Although the church was built earlier, the first resident pastor was assigned to the parish in 1854, which may account for this anniversary date. (Ernie DeFronzo.)

CENTURY CELEBRATION, 1954. Parishioners gather for an anniversary picture in front of the brick facade and stained-glass windows of old Saint Mary's Stony Hill. Many early township residents are buried in Saint Mary's Stony Hill Cemetery, which remains on the Plainfield Avenue property. (Ernie DeFronzo.)

"THIS IS THE WAY WE WASH OUR CLOTHES," c. 1910. Mountain Avenue resident Louise Crowe Swaysland seems unfazed by the drudgery of doing laundry with only a washboard for help. (Rita Ragno.)

HAPPY BIRTHDAY, MARGIE!, 1942. Resplendent in birthday bonnets, township friends from the Snyder Avenue area celebrate Marjorie Spangenberg's birthday. Guests are, from left to right: (front row) unidentified, Carol Drake, Margie (the birthday girl), Eleanor Crockett, and Jane Larson; (back row) Bill Gemmil, Evelyn Knoop, Emily Plummer, and Sonny Spangenberg. (Carol Drake Friedman.)

116

COMMUNITY HOUSE, 1925. In 1918 a group of residents organized a social and cultural association and raised funds to build this community house on Plainfield Avenue. The club sponsored lectures, flower shows, musicals, movies, and dances until after World War II. Now a two-family home, the building is easily recognized by its broad facade and expansive roof line. (Rita Ragno.)

WOMEN'S AUXILIARY, COMMUNITY HOUSE, c. late 1930s. From left to right are: (front row) Hortense Hallock, Ella Gehrig, Lillian Shaffer, Olga Curtis, Charlotte Burgmiller, Lillian Staats, Gertrude Moore, and Gladys Couser; (back row) Annie J. Shaffer, Marion Boaté, Ruby Rogers, Emily Crowe, Mae Wilson, Helen Legge, Grace Moore, Virginia Vandereof, Mildred Shaffer, Emily McLeod, unidentified, Ruth Griffin, Jean Mulholland, and Helen Moore. (Gail Shaffer.)

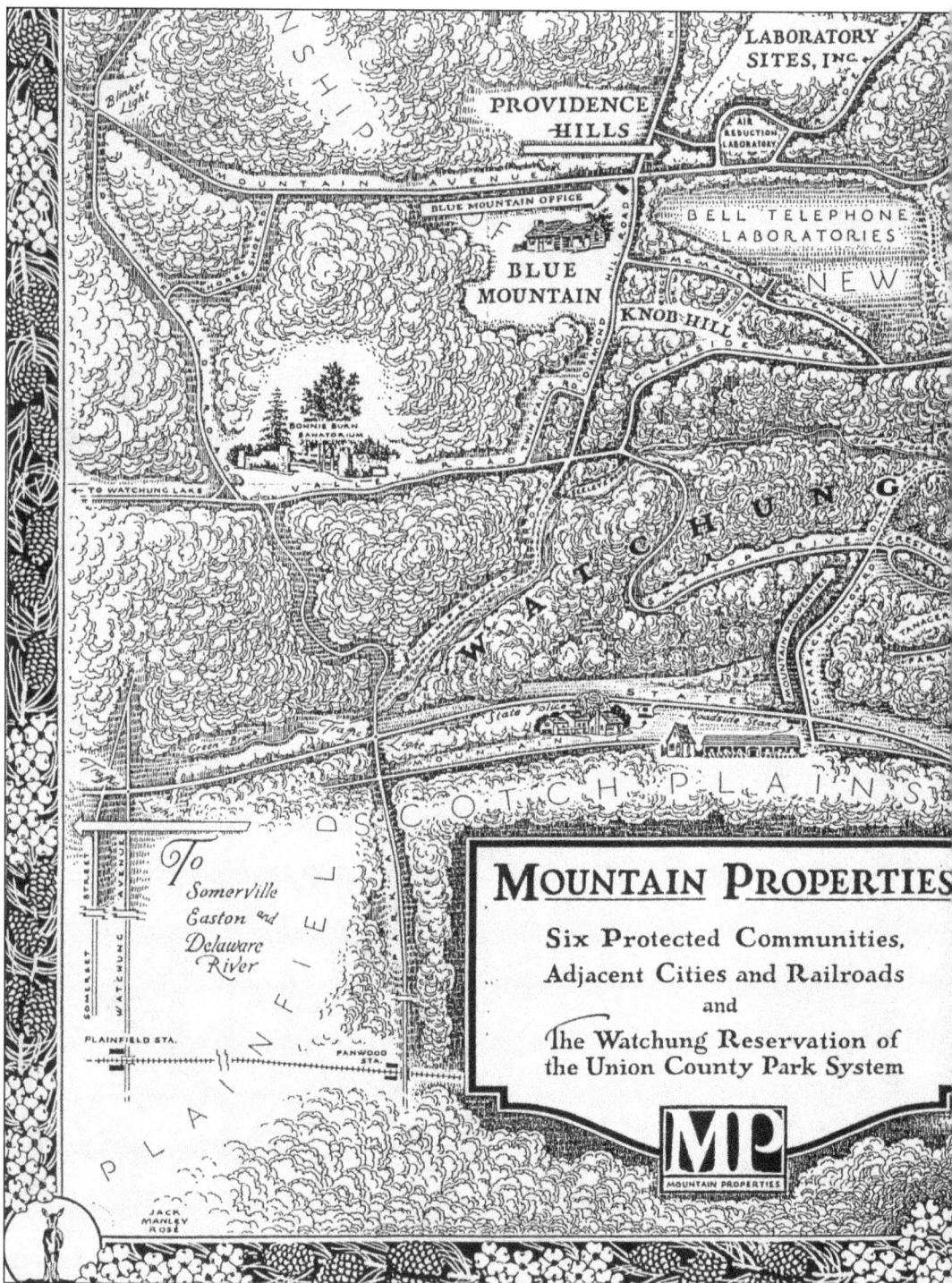

MOUNTAIN PROPERTIES, c. 1945. This section of a real estate map drawn by Summit artist Jack Manley Rosé, who painted the lobby mural at the Playhouse in Summit, shows the locations of proposed housing developments in the vicinity of the Watchung Reservation. The late Edward Grassman, a longtime area resident, owned part of the property. Several model

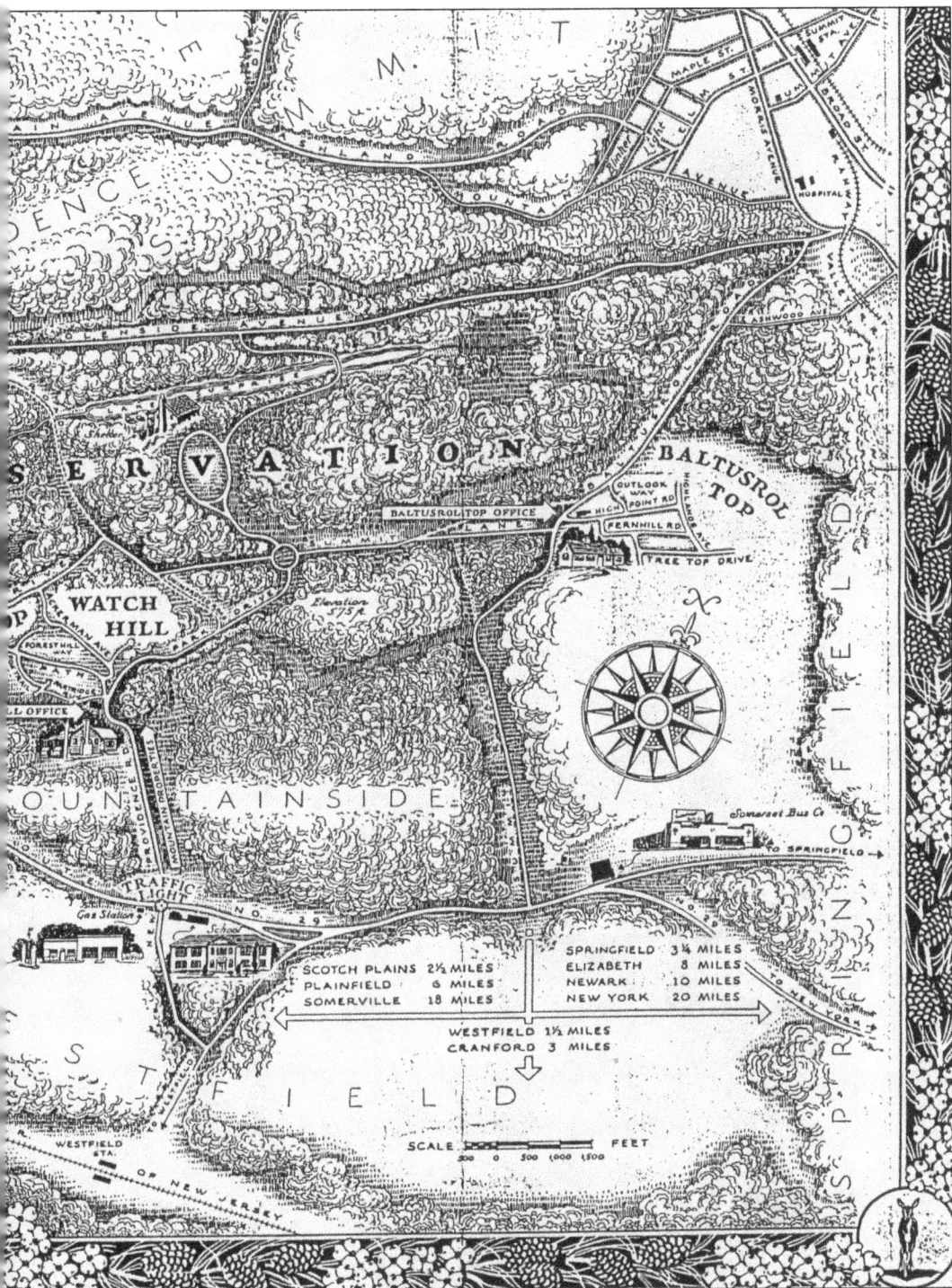

homes were available in the Blue Mountain Farms section on Twin Falls Road in Berkeley Heights. The architectural firm of McMurray and Schmidlin won an award for their designs of these affordable, attractive houses. (Virginia Troeger.)

HONOR ROLL PARADE, c. 1943. Red Cross workers and other residents march to town hall for the unveiling of the Berkeley Heights Honor Roll, which listed the men and women from the area serving in World War II. Berkeley Heights was officially known as New Providence Township at this time. (Bo Bosefskie.)

WORLD WAR II HONOR ROLL, c. 1943. From left to right are: Berkeley Heights Mayor Anton C. Swenson, Mrs. P.L. Proctor (of the local Red Cross), Township Committee Member H.M. Kent, and Judge Joseph Mulholland. The group is viewing the newly unveiled Berkeley Heights Honor Roll. (Bo Bosefskie.)

WIN WITH TIN!, c. 1943. Members of the England-Kuntz families, Boy Scouts, and other residents collect scrap metal and rubber tires at town hall to be recycled into war materials. Founded in 1922, the A.W. Kuntz Recreation Construction Company sold a product called "Beam Clay" used to construct tennis courts, baseball fields, and horse-stall floors at race tracks. (Bo Bosefskie.)

V-J DAY PARADE, 1945. Joyous Berkeley Heights citizens parade on Plainfield Avenue past Mount Carmel Hall (now the Berkeley Heights Public Library) to celebrate the end of World War II. (Gail Shaffer.)

HIGHLANDERS, 1903. The Berkeley Heights Athletic Club played competitive baseball in the Lackawanna League, which was composed of teams in towns along the railroad. From left to right are: (front row) Louis Burgmiller Jr., J. Anson, F. Cope, and Frank Exner; (back row) William Burgmiller, Felix Layat, Rob Rogers, Louis Funk, Charles Burgmiller, and Ben Debbie. (Gail Shaffer.)

COLUMBIA SCHOOL TEAM, c. 1930. Supervising Principal William Woodruff stands with his baseball team—baseball was the only sport offered at the school. From left to right are: (front row) William Stonecipher, James Monica, Leonard England, Michael Mondelli, William D. Russo, James LaSasso, and bat boy Frank Fornaro; (back row) Louis Del Gaudio, Harold Curtis, Dominick Campano, and Edward Campano. (Berkeley Heights Historical Society.)

BERKELEY BRAVES, 1948. Players on this local team were, from left to right: (front row) John Turiano, Nick DeFronzo, Dan Russo, Mascot Red Larson, George Kolb, and Bob Rogers; (back row) Walter Holley, Ralph Del Duca, Ernie DeFronzo, Tom Mazzucco, Art Larson, and Bob McCusker. (Ernie DeFronzo.)

P.A.L. BASEBALL, c. 1950. Police Athletic League baseball was started in town in the 1950s. Shown here are the elementary school players on one of the first teams. From left to right are: (front row) J. Natale, M. Delia, P. McCloud, S. Imbimbi, P. Schwartz, and unidentified; (back row) Assistant Coach P. Phillippi, B. Nigro, N. Seritelli, J. Phillippi, F. Vicendese, and Coach P. England. (Bo Bosefskie.)

LITTELL-LORD FARMHOUSE, *c*. 1970. Home of the Berkeley Heights Historical Society and public museum since the late 1970s, 31 Horseshoe Road was built about 1760 by Andrew Littell, a farmer and weaver. He lived in the house with his wife Mary and their seven children, until his death in 1790. Other owners followed until the Lord family bought the house in 1867. They added the Victorian annex next door (pictured on the opposite page), built in the Carpenter Gothic style. The annex was used in the 1870s as a school. Elizabeth Wemett, the last of the Lord family to live on the property, sold it to the township in 1975. The entire farmstead has been placed on the State and National Registers of Historic Places. (Berkeley Heights Historical Society.)

NUMBER 23 HORSESHOE ROAD. *See opposite page.* (Berkeley Heights Historical Society.)

HORSESHOE ROAD AT MOUNTAIN AVENUE, 1959. The Lord family barn on the right hides the Littell-Lord farmhouse and the Victorian house next door. The barn, which may have been an original building on the property, was taken down in 1976. (Bo Bosefskie.)

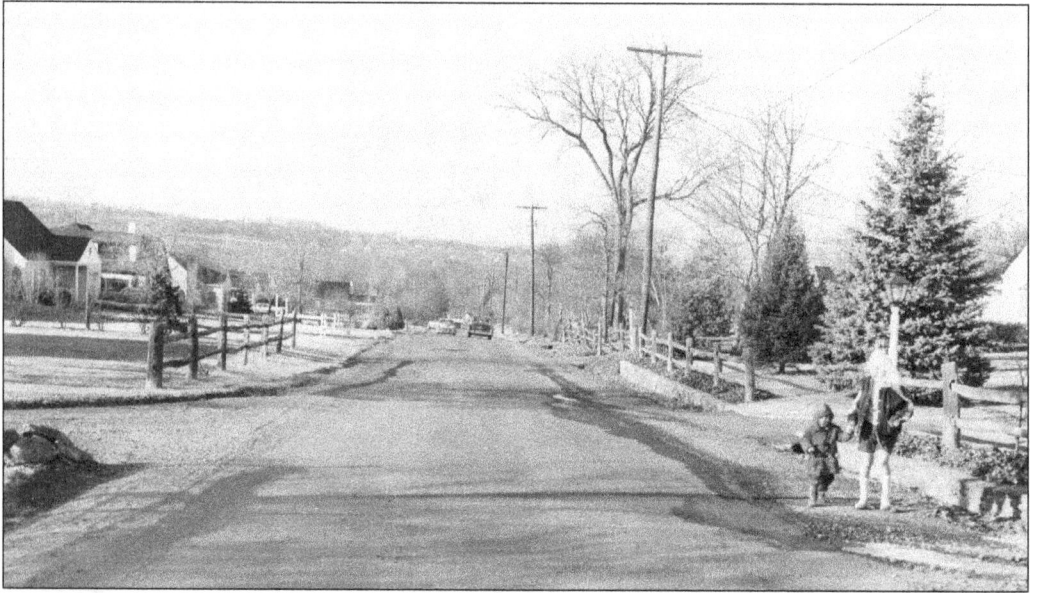

DOGWOOD LANE, FACING NORTH, 1959. The photographs on these two pages and the Lord family barn photograph on the preceding page are a few of the more than one hundred engineering department photographs taken before the installation of sanitary sewers in town. Two employees found these photographs tucked away in a cardboard box at the water treatment department, probably unseen for more than thirty years. (Bo Bosefskie.)

ROGERS PLACE, FEBRUARY 1959. Except for the antique cars and the box for the *Newark News* (which ceased publication in 1972), much remains the same at this corner. Rogers Place was named for the Rogers family, who lived in the area for many years. The Rogers and Shaffer General Store was located on the right on what is now the site of a professional building. (Bo Bosefskie.)

126

BERKSHIRE DRIVE FACING MOUNTAIN AVENUE, FEBRUARY 1959. In the 1830s, Balthasar Oechsner (later spelled Exner), an early settler from Germany, purchased all the land on both sides of Stony Hill Road (Mountain Avenue) from Diamond Hill Road to beyond Snyder Avenue. Oechsner Court off Mountain Avenue near Timber Drive commemorates the family. (Bo Bosefskie.)

GOODBYE SEPTIC TANKS!, MAY 1959. A worker from Carbet Sewer Contractors installs a sewer manhole structure on Oakland Street. After World War II, Berkeley Heights experienced a home building boom which, by the end of the 1950s, required the installation of city sewers to replace septic tanks. (Bo Bosefskie.)

WOMAN'S CLUB TEA, c. 1965. Members of the Berkeley Heights Woman's Club, Mrs. Lloyd Krieger-Hueber (left) and Mrs. Leon P. Sudrabin (right) enjoy a festive afternoon tea (the woman in the center has not been identified). The club was founded in 1955 and continues today as a vital organization of eighty women, pursuing goals in education, national and world affairs, the arts, and community service. (Berkeley Heights Woman's Club.)

Select Bibliography

Bierbaum, Martin A. "Free Acres: Bolton Hall's Single-Tax Experimental Community." *New Jersey History*, Volume 102, Number 1-2 (Spring/Summer 1984).

Desmond, Helen E., ed. *From the Passaiack to the Wach Unks, A History of the Township of Berkeley Heights, New Jersey*. Berkeley Heights, NJ: The Historical Society of Berkeley Heights, 1977.

Hawley, James B. *The Deserted Village and The Blue Brook Valley*. Illustrated by Mr. and Mrs. Walter J. Young. Mountainside, NJ: Trailside Museum Association, 1964.

Gregor, Arthur. *Bell Laboratories, Inside the World's Largest Communication Center*. New York: Charles Scribner's Sons, 1977.

Romano, Joseph Albert. *Free Acres Single Tax Colony, 1910–1930: An Experiment in Pleasant Living*. A thesis presented to the Graduate Council of the University of Tennessee in partial fulfillment of the requirements for the Master of Arts Degree, 1972.

www.ingramcontent.com/pod-product-compliance
Lightning Source LLC
Chambersburg PA
CBHW080849100426
42812CB00007B/1971